nF419081

# "Smart Cities: The Technology Transforming Urban Living"

# Table of Contents

# Copyright Notice

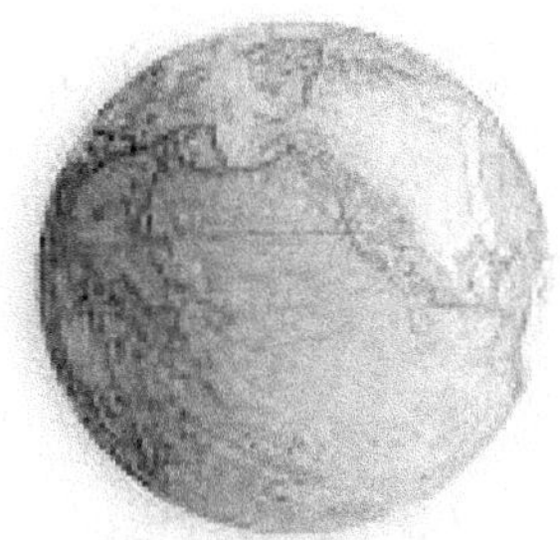

## **All Rights Reserved.**

No part of this publication may be reproduced, or stored in a database or retrieval system, or transmitted, in any form or by any means, electronic, mechanical, photocopying, recording, or otherwise, without the prior written permission of the publisher. No patent liability is assumed with respect to the use of the information contained herein.

Although every precaution has been taken in the preparation of this book, the author and publisher assume no responsibility for the errors or omissions. Neither is any liability assumed resulting from the use of the information contained herein.

**Copyright 2024©** Dr. Patrick Mukosha

**First published:** July, 2024
**Publisher**: Patrick Mukosha PhD

## Trademarks

All terms mentioned in this book that are known to be trademarks or service marks have been appropriately capitalized. The Author and the publisher cannot attest to the accuracy of this information. Use of a term in this book should not be regarded as affecting the validity of any trademark or service mark.

## Warning and Disclaimer

Every effort has been made to make this book as complete and as accurate as possible, but no warranty or fitness is implied. The information provided in this book is on as is basis. The Author and the Publisher shall have neither liability nor responsibility to any person or entity with respect to any loss or damage arising from the use the information contained in this book.

**Author:**  Dr. Patrick Chisenga Mukosha

# Acknowledgements

The author is indebted to a large number of researchers, and consultants in the field of Information Technology, Infrastructure and Urban Planning, Internet of Things, whose works were referred to in writing this book – and appears below and in the bibliography.

The author also would like to acknowledge the encouragement of my wife; Gracious Lumba Maboshe-Mukosha, and my children, whose comments and constructive criticism kept the author alive. The author also benefitted from the comments of several of my Infrastructure and Urban Planning and ICT colleagues. They generously shared their insights and experiences in an evolving field where tacit knowledge is indispensable.

Special thanks go to Lionel Hugh Weston; an Educationalist, British National, my former Secondary School Teacher and Guardian, without whom I would never have had a strong education foundation in life. His contribution in my education career is immeasurable. I shall forever remain indebted to him and the entire Weston's family.

## Abstract

IT specialist; Dr. Patrick Mukosha, explores the transformative effects of technology on urban surroundings in **"Smart Cities: *The Technology Transforming Urban Living.*"** With almost two-thirds of the world's population expected to reside in cities by 2050, urbanization is expected to continue accelerating and bring both enormous opportunities and concerns. This book offers a *thorough examination of the ways in which innovative technologies are transforming urban life and improving the efficiency, sustainability, and livability of cities.*

The trip starts with a thoughtful *introduction to the idea of smart cities*, outlining their development and importance in the modern world. *Readers are introduced to the technical pillars supporting smart cities,* from Artificial Intelligence (AI) to the Internet of Things (IoT), demonstrating how these breakthroughs gather and analyze data to improve many aspects of city living.

Smart cities are *revolutionizing transportation through the use of driverless vehicles, sophisticated traffic management, and public transit systems that reduce traffic and increase mobility.* Smart collection systems and waste-to-energy technology are two examples of *intelligent waste management solutions* that show how cities may become greener and more sustainable.

The book also examines how *technology is revolutionizing healthcare, with telemedicine, remote monitoring, and health data analytics enhancing patient access and tailored treatment.* With smart classrooms, e-learning platforms, and measures to bridge the digital gap. E-government services rethink governance and citizen participation.

Finally, the book looks ahead, *examining new technologies and the development of smart cities while highlighting the significance of resilience, adaptability, and human-centered design.*

For anyone interested in the future of urban living, **"Smart Cities: *The Technology Transforming Urban Living"*** is an engaging and educational read.

# Chapter 1: Introduction to Smart Cities

## 1.1. Defining Smart Cities

A *Smart City* is basically, an urban area where data collecting and technology are used to enhance the sustainability and efficiency of city operations, as well as the quality of life. Local governments use Internet of Things (IoT) and Information and Communication Technology (ICT) in smart cities. However, below is a broader definition of a smart city which we shall embrace throughout this book.

> **Definition:** *Smart Cities are metropolitan areas that use data-driven solutions and cutting-edge technology to improve resident quality of life, increase operational efficiency, and encourage sustainable growth. Smart cities seek to address the issues brought on by increasing urbanization, resource restrictions, and climate change by incorporating Information and Communication Technologies (ICT) and Internet of Things (IoT) into routine city tasks –* **Patrick Mukosha***.*

Smart infrastructure, Internet of Things (IoT) devices, big data analytics, artificial intelligence (AI), sustainable energy solutions, intelligent transportation systems, and improved public services are some of the essential elements of smart cities. Together, these elements provide an urban environment that is responsive, unified, and flexible.

### 1.1.1. **Essential Elements of Smart Cities**:

1. **Smart Infrastructure**: Refers to the effective monitoring and management of resources by integrating sensors and connectivity into roadways, buildings, and other structures.
2. **IoT Integration**: Is the process of integrating systems and sensors to gather data in real time on a variety of urban issues, including energy use, traffic, and air quality.
3. **Big Data & Analytics:** Applying data analytics to make better decisions and obtain insights to enhance resident services and city operations.
4. **Artificial Intelligence:** Using AI to automate operations, anticipate trends, and improve procedures will increase the responsiveness and efficiency of the city.

5. **Sustainable Energy:** Is the use of smart grids and renewable energy sources to lessen environmental effect and increase energy efficiency.
6. **Smart Transportation:** Refers to the development of driverless cars, intelligent public transportation, and dynamic traffic control to increase efficiency and lessen traffic.
7. **Enhanced Public Services:** Using technology to raise public safety, waste management, healthcare, and education standards, as well as to make cities more resilient and habitable.

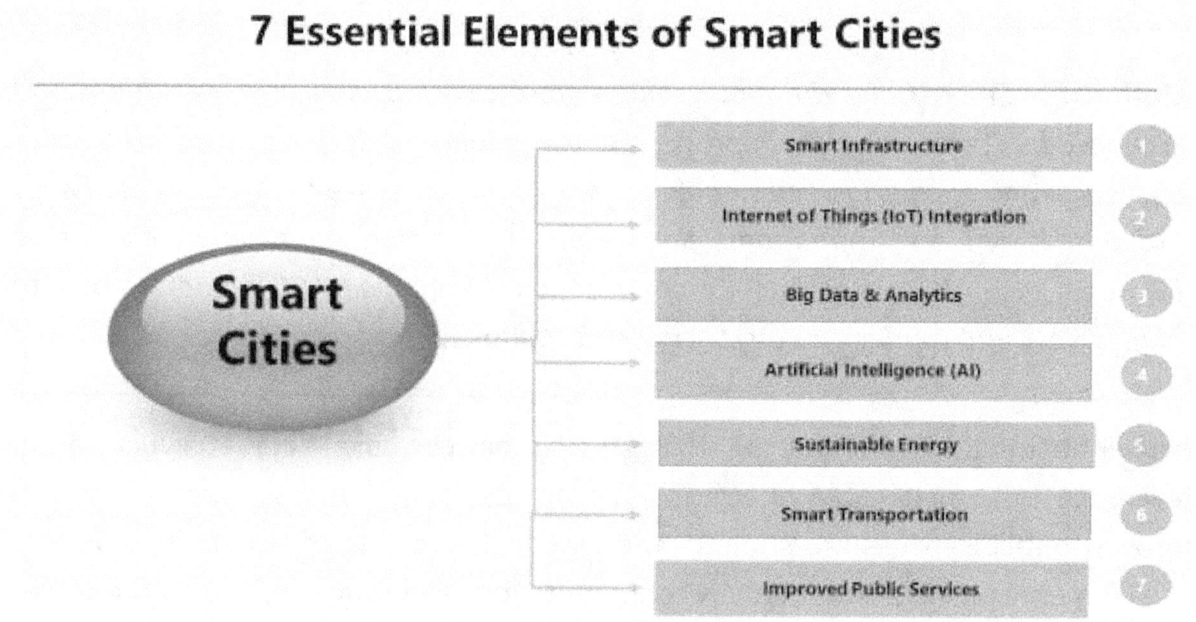

**Source:** Smart Cities: *The Technology Transforming Urban Living,* GoodMan Series, (Patrick Mukosha, 2024).

*Figure 1: 7 Essential Elements of Smart Cities*

In summary, smart cities, which combine cutting-edge technology with data-driven solutions, provide a revolutionary way to live in cities. Smart city programs have a wide range of uses and benefits, as demonstrated by the following examples: Singapore, Barcelona, Amsterdam, New York City, and others. Smart cities seek to build inclusive, technologically sophisticated urban settings that are also sensitive to the demands of their citizens by emphasizing sustainability, efficiency, and public participation.

A smart city is a technologically advanced metropolitan region that gathers specialized data using various electrical systems and sensors. The data is used to enhance operations throughout the city by providing information that is utilized to manage resources, assets, and services effectively. In order to monitor and manage traffic and transportation systems, power plants, utilities, urban forestry, water supply networks, waste, criminal investigations, information systems, schools, libraries, hospitals, and other community services, data is gathered from citizens, devices, buildings, and assets. This data is then processed and analyzed.

Smart cities are characterized by their governments' use of technology and by the way they monitor, assess, organize, and run the city. *In smart cities, companies, residents, and other outside parties that may gain from different applications of the data are sharing it with the city as a whole.* When data from many systems and industries are shared, there are chances for better understanding and financial gains.

In order to maximize the effectiveness of city operations and services and establish a connection with inhabitants, *the smart city idea combines information and communication technology (ICT) with a variety of physical devices linked to the Internet of things (IOT) network.* With the use of smart city technology, local government representatives can monitor the city's activities and changes while also having direct communication with the public and city infrastructure. ICT is utilized to improve urban services' performance, quality, and interactivity; lower expenses and resource consumption; and foster closer ties between the public and the government.

Applications for smart cities are created to control urban flows and enable real-time reactions. Therefore, *a smart city might be better equipped to handle problems than a city with traditional "transactional" ties to its residents.* However, the term itself is still ambiguous and so susceptible to several meanings. Smart city technology has already been used in many cities. Around the world, hundreds of smart city initiatives are presently under development. Initiatives aimed at creating "*Smarter Cities*" seek to improve citizen services, monitor and optimize current infrastructure, foster more cooperation between various economic actors, and support creative business models in the public and private domains. *The ultimate goal of smart cities is to make their local communities more competitive.*

Similar to how the nervous system of the body controls how people react to their surroundings, developing technologies are giving cities the ability to adapt to changes in their own urban environments. Initiatives to create smart cities and reap the benefits they offer depend heavily on data collection technologies, notably real-time data. Data-driven insights assist local governments in enhancing urban planning and the implementation of city services, such as public transit and garbage management, which enhances the quality of life for citizens.

Enhancing local air quality and reducing carbon emissions are two more ways that more effective city services may support international efforts to combat climate change. Additionally, as improved infrastructure and technological advancements can promote job creation and commercial opportunities, smart city solutions can be a catalyst for economic growth.

Essentially, smart communities and cities have three distinguishing characteristics:

- **Connectivity**: Municipal officials can monitor and manage city infrastructure and have direct community interactions because to connectivity.
- **Accessible Data**: The public is frequently given access to operations and planning data by the local government, which is dedicated to the open data movement.
- **Networks:** Sensor networks collect and process data for use in a variety of applications and city services, by use of the Internet of Things (IoT).

## 1.3. Smart City Technologies

As stated earlier on, the term "*Smart City Technologies*" refers to a *collection of cutting-edge digital tools and systems intended to enhance urban living by increasing a city's sustainability, efficiency, and responsiveness to its citizens' demands.* These technologies improve public services, infrastructure, transportation, energy management, citizen involvement, and many other areas of city life by utilizing the Internet of Things (IoT), big data, artificial intelligence (AI), and advanced communication networks.

### 1.3.1. Important Smart City Technologies with Illustrations

#### 1.3.1.1. Internet of Things (IoT)

- **Definition:** In order to gather and share data, IoT devices—such as sensors and actuators—are connected to the internet.
- **Examples:**

- o **Smart Streetlights:** To save energy and enhance public safety, cities like Los Angeles have installed smart street lighting systems that change brightness in response to car and pedestrian movement.
- o **Environmental Sensors:** Internet of Things (IoT) sensors track temperature, noise levels, and air quality in cities like Chicago. They provide real-time data that aids in the management of urban pollution and public health.

### 1.3.1.2. Big Data Analytics

- **Definition:** In order to gain valuable insights and guide decision-making, big data analytics entails processing and analyzing massive amounts of data.
- **Examples:**
  - o **Predictive Policing**: To pinpoint crime hotspots and more efficiently deploy police resources, New York City uses big data analytics.
  - o **Urban Planning:** Land use planning is optimized and urban growth scenarios are simulated in Singapore through the application of big data analytics.

### 1.3.1.3. Artificial Intelligence (AI)

- **Definition:** AI refers to technologies that make it possible for machines to carry out tasks like learning, reasoning, and problem-solving that normally need human intelligence.
- **Examples:**
  - o **Traffic Management:** Barcelona employs artificial intelligence (AI) to dynamically control traffic signals, which eases congestion and enhances traffic flow.
  - o **Waste Management**: AI-driven systems in Copenhagen optimize waste collection routes by using data from smart bins in real-time, which boosts productivity and lowers operating expenses.

### 1.3.1.4. Advanced Communication Networks (5G):

- **Definition:** 5G and other advanced communication networks offer high-speed, low-latency connection that is necessary for real-time data transmission and applications related to smart cities.
- **Examples:**

- o **Smart Mobility**: By enabling connected public transportation systems and driverless cars, Seoul's 5G network enhances both the safety and effectiveness of transportation.
- o **Public Safety:** 5G makes it possible for real-time video surveillance and quick emergency response in London.

1.3.1.5. **Smart Grids:**

- **Definition:** To increase efficiency and dependability, smart grids are electrical networks that employ digital communications technology to recognize and respond to changes in local consumption.
- **Examples:**
  - o **Energy Management:** Demand response is used by Amsterdam's smart grid to balance supply and demand, minimizing energy waste, and it incorporates renewable energy sources like wind and solar power.
  - o **Outage Management**: Chattanooga's smart grid system reduces downtime and enhances service dependability by swiftly isolating and resolving power outages.

1.3.1.6. **Intelligent Transportation Systems (ITS):**

- **Definition:** ITS uses cutting-edge technology to improve efficiency, safety, and traffic control in transportation systems.
- **Examples:**
  - o **Smart Public Transportation:** To ensure precise arrival times, optimize routes, and effectively manage fleet operations, Singapore's public transportation system leverages real-time data.
  - o **Autonomous Vehicles:** In Silicon Valley, businesses are testing self-driving cars and shuttles that traverse urban areas using a mix of artificial intelligence, GPS, and sensors.

1.3.1.7. **E-Government Services:**

- **Definition:** E-government services refer to the more transparent and efficient delivery of public services via the use of digital technologies.
- **Examples:**
  - o **Digital Citizen Services:** By enabling online access to government services from any location, businesses and people in

Estonia can benefit from increased convenience and efficiency thanks to the e-residency program.

- ○ **Participatory Platforms:** To promote better transparency and involvement, Paris employs platforms such as "Madame Mayor, I Have an Idea" to involve residents in decision-making processes.

1.3.1.8. **Sustainable Energy Solutions:**

- **Definition:** To lower carbon emissions and increase energy efficiency, sustainable energy solutions incorporate renewable energy sources and technology.

- **Examples:**
  - ○ **Solar Energy:** San Francisco has greatly reduced its carbon footprint by installing solar panels on public buildings and offering incentives to citizens to switch to solar power.
  - ○ **Energy-Efficient Buildings:** In order to encourage sustainable urban growth, Vancouver has implemented strict building laws that mandate new projects adhere to high energy efficiency standards.

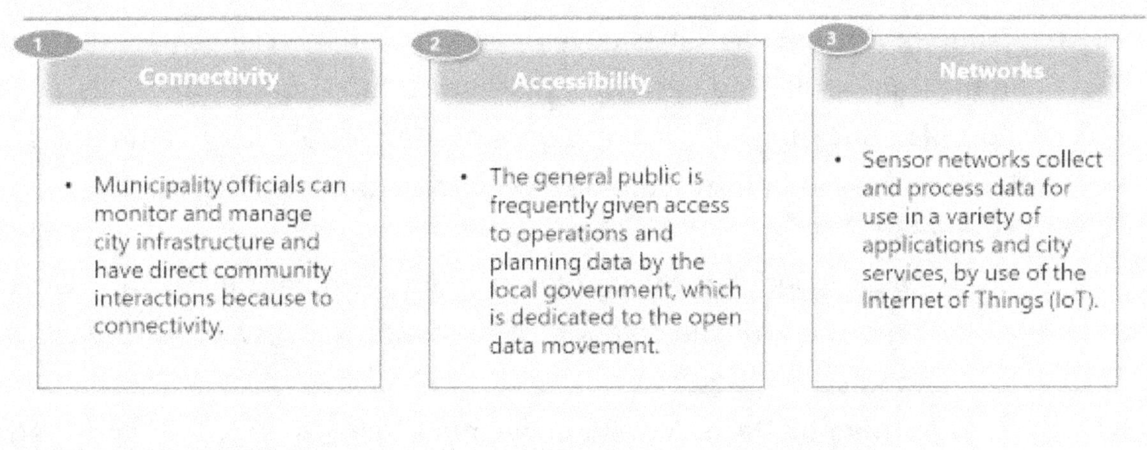



**Source:** Smart Cities: *The Technology Transforming Urban Living*, GoodMan Series, (Patrick Mukosha, 2024).

*Figure 2: 3 Distinct Characteristics of Smart Cities*

In summary, urban settings are changing as a result of smart city technology, which increase their interconnectedness, efficiency, and resident-responsiveness. Global cities are confronting the issues of urbanization and building more livable, sustainable, and resilient communities by integrating IoT, big data, AI, advanced communication networks, smart grids, ITS, e-government services, and sustainable energy solutions.

## 1.4. The Evolution of Urbanization

Over millennia, the dynamic process of urbanization has changed both human communities and the physical environments of cities. Comprehending the progression of urbanization offers essential background information for the creation and application of smart city technologies. This section examines the major stages in the development of urbanization and identifies the forces behind this change.

**1.4.1. Historic Urban Areas:** In areas like Mesopotamia (modern-day Iraq), the Indus Valley (modern-day Pakistan and India), and Egypt, the earliest towns are believed to have existed circa 4000 BCE.

These early cities have the following characteristics:

    a. **Agricultural Surplus:** The introduction of agriculture led to the creation of excess food, which in turn enabled the growth of larger, longer-lasting towns.

    b. **Trade & Commerce:** Cities developed into commercial centers that aided in the transfer of products, concepts, and cultural norms.

    c. **Complex Societies:** Urban areas gave rise to centralized government, social hierarchies, and infrastructure like water and granary systems.

    d. **Example:**

        o **Uruk**: One of Mesopotamia's first significant towns, Uruk is renowned for the creation of the first writing systems as well as its magnificent ziggurats.

        o **Mohenjo-Daro:** A well-known Indus Valley metropolis renowned for its cutting-edge drainage and urban planning techniques.

1.4.2. **Middle Ages and Renaissance Urbanisation:** Urbanization slowed down in many parts of the world throughout the medieval era (5th to 15th century) for a variety of reasons, including the fall of the Roman Empire and the rise of Feudalism. Nonetheless, cities started to prosper once more throughout the Renaissance (the 14th to the 17th century), propelled by:

a. **Economic Revival:** Rich merchant cities arose as a result of the resurgence of trade routes and the expansion of business.

b. **Cultural and Scientific Advancements**: Cities developed into hubs of knowledge and creativity, which supported the artistic and scientific accomplishments of the Renaissance.

c. **Better Roads, Bridges, and Buildings:** To accommodate the expanding urban population, better roads, bridges, and buildings were built.

d. **Example:**
   - **Florence:** Known for its contributions to science, art, and architecture, Florence was a major Renaissance metropolis.
   - **Venice**: Is a significant hub of trade and culture that is well-known for its waterways and nautical skill.

1.4.3. **Contemporary Urbanization and the Industrial Revolution:** In the history of urbanization, the Industrial Revolution (18th and 19th centuries) was a pivotal moment. Important elements comprised:

a. **Industrialization:** A vast number of people moved to cities in search of work as factories and mechanized production grew.

b. **Transportation Innovations:** The rise of cities was accelerated by the construction of railroads, steamships, and eventually vehicles, which made it easier to move people and products.

c. **Urban Infrastructure:** As cities grew quickly, new networks of public transit, electricity, and sewer systems were created to accommodate the expanding populations.

d. **Example:**
   - **Manchester:** Dubbed the "first industrial city," Manchester's explosive expansion during the Industrial Revolution is a prime example of how industrialization changed urban environments.
   - **City of New York:** It became a global city with the building of skyscrapers and massive infrastructure in the late 19th and early 20th centuries.

1.4.4. **Urbanization Following World War II:** In the years after World War II, there was an unparalleled surge in urbanization, especially in the developed world, propelled by:

a. **Economic Boom:** Greater urbanization and suburbanization were brought about by the post-war economic boom, especially in the United States and Western Europe.

b. **Technological Advancements:** The growth and modernization of cities were made possible by breakthroughs in the fields of building, transportation, and communication.

c. **Globalization**: The development of important urban centers as hubs for the economy and culture was facilitated by the expansion of international trade and multinational enterprises.

d. **Example:**
- **Tokyo:** After World War II, Tokyo was rapidly rebuilt and expanded, and it came to represent post-war urbanization and economic progress.
- **Los Angeles:** Known for its vast freeway system and suburban sprawl, Los Angeles reflects post-war American urbanization patterns.

1.4.5. **The Rise of Smart Cities in the 21st Century:** Over half of the world's population currently resides in urban regions as a result of the rapid urbanization that has continued throughout the twenty-first century. This stage is distinguished by:

a. **Sustainable Development:** Reducing the environmental effect of cities and placing more emphasis on sustainable urban planning are two aspects of sustainable development.

b. **Digital Transformation:** Is the process of integrating technological advancements like big data, artificial intelligence, and the Internet of Things to build smarter, more resilient, and habitable cities.

c. **Global Urban Networks:** Cities are becoming more interconnected through international networks, which makes it easier to share best practices, technology, and expertise.

d. **Example:**
- **Singapore**: Is a model smart city that uses technology to enhance sustainability and urban living.
- **Barcelona:** Well-known for its smart city programs that improve living conditions and encourage participation from the public.

In summary, urbanization's development is evidence of humanity's capacity for innovation and adaptation in the face of shifting social, technological, and economic circumstances.

Every stage of urbanization, from prehistoric urban centers to contemporary smart cities, has built on the one before it, resulting in today's cities that use technology to solve problems of the modern world and enhance urban living. To fully appreciate the potential and significance of smart city technologies in influencing the future of urban living, it is imperative to comprehend this historical background.

## 1.5. Importance of Smart Cities in Modern Society

The notion of smart cities has surfaced as a crucial reaction to the diverse obstacles encountered by metropolitan regions in the 21st century. The demand on resources, services, and infrastructure rises as more people relocate to urban areas. Smart cities use technology to improve urban living and maintain livability, sustainability, and economic vibrancy. Here, we examine the complex role that smart cities play in contemporary society.

### 1.5.1. **Improving Quality of Life:**
#### 1.5.1.1. **Important Points:**
   a. **Improved Services**: Smart cities use digital platforms to provide improved public services, like online health services, real-time public transportation updates, and e-government services. Residents now have easier access to and use of these services.
   b. **Health and Safety:** Medical services are improved by the use of cutting-edge healthcare technologies including telemedicine and health monitoring systems. Public safety is enhanced by smart monitoring and emergency response systems.
   c. **Example:**
      o **Barcelona:** Uses effective public transportation and smart waste management, which results in cleaner streets and more mobility for locals.
      o **Singapore:** Offers top-notch healthcare services by using AI and IoT to monitor and address public health issues.

### 1.5.2. **Encouraging Sustainability:**
#### 1.5.2.1. **Important Points:**
   a. **Energy Efficiency:** Carbon footprints are decreased, renewable energy sources are integrated, and energy use is optimized through smart grids and energy management systems.

b. **Environmental Monitoring:** Cities may prevent pollution and environmental degradation by using sensors to monitor air and water quality, noise levels, and other environmental parameters.

c. **Example:**
   - **Amsterdam:** Uses renewable energy sources and smart grid integration to control energy consumption.
   - **Copenhagen:** Modifies traffic patterns to cut emissions and uses Internet of Things sensors to track air quality.

### 1.5.3. Innovation and Economic Growth

### 1.5.3.1.  Important Points:

a. **Attracting Businesses:** Modern infrastructure and effective urban planning draw companies and capital, which promotes economic expansion.

b. **Employment Creation**: New positions in IT, engineering, urban planning, and related sectors are generated by the development and upkeep of smart city technologies.

c. **Example:**
   - **Zhejiang Province (Hangzhou):** The home of *Alibaba*, the city draws tech firms and startups with its cutting-edge digital infrastructure, creating a thriving innovation ecosystem.
   - **London:** The city's open data efforts stimulate economic growth by fostering entrepreneurship and innovation.

### 1.5.4. Effective Management of Resources

### 1.5.4.1.  Important Points:

a. **Water Management:** To ensure effective use of water resources, smart water systems monitor usage, identify leaks, and optimize distribution.

b. **Waste Management:** Recycling rates are increased and waste management expenses are decreased with IoT-enabled waste bins and intelligent pickup routes.

c. **Example:**
   - **Paris:** Reduces environmental effect and optimizes collection schedules using smart garbage containers.

- o **New York City:** Smart water meters are being used in New York City to better control water use and find leaks.

## 1.5.5. Enhanced Mobility in Cities

### 1.5.5.1. Important Points:

a. **Smart Transportation:** Intelligent transportation systems, or "*Smart Transportation*," control traffic, ease congestion, and encourage the use of public transportation.

b. **Autonomous Vehicles:** The advancement of smart traffic management systems and self-driving automobiles improves road safety and lessens traffic congestion.

c. **Example:**

- o **Seoul:** To increase general mobility, traffic signals and public transportation schedules are managed by AI and IoT.
- o **Los Angeles:** Putting autonomous car testing into practice to provide safer and more effective transit options.

## 1.5.6. Better Citizen Engagement and Governance

### 1.5.6.1. Important Points:

a. **E-Government Services:** By streamlining government functions through digital platforms, citizens may access and utilize them more effectively.

b. **Public Participation:** Smart cities promote public participation by providing forums for locals to express their thoughts and get involved in urban development.

c. **Example:**

- o **Estonia:** Provides a wide range of e-government services that encourage citizen participation in governance and expedite administrative procedures.
- o **Paris:** To promote participatory democracy, the "*Madame Mayor, I Have an Idea*" platform allows residents to suggest and vote on public projects.

## 1.5.7. Adaptability and Resilience

### 1.5.7.1. Important Points:

a. **Disaster Management:** To improve emergency response and disaster management capabilities, smart cities make use of real-time data and predictive analytics.

b. **Climate Adaptation:** Cities can lessen the consequences of climate change and adapt to it by using technologies that monitor and control environmental conditions.

c. **Example:**
   - **Tokyo:** To manage natural calamities, the city has a sophisticated early warning system for earthquakes and robust infrastructure.
   - **New Orleans:** Smart flood management technologies are being implemented in New Orleans in order to guard against hurricanes and sea level rise.

In summary, one cannot exaggerate the significance of smart cities in contemporary culture. Smart cities solve the urgent issues of urbanization, improve quality of life, encourage sustainability, spur economic growth, and guarantee effective resource management by incorporating cutting-edge technologies into urban design and management. Furthermore, smart cities encourage increased resilience and public engagement, which better prepares them to meet difficulties in the future. The creation and growth of smart cities will be essential in determining sustainable and habitable urban settings for future generations as urban populations continue to rise.

# Chapter 2: The Backbone of Smart Cities: Infrastructure and Urban Planning

## 2.1. Smart Infrastructure: An Overview

The term "*Smart Infrastructure*" describes the incorporation of cutting-edge systems and technology into rural and urban infrastructure to improve sustainability, efficiency, and quality of life. To monitor and optimize infrastructure systems like waste management, electricity, water, and transportation, sensors, data analytics, and networking are used.

### 2.1.1. Important Elements of Smart Infrastructure:

#### 2.1.1.1. IoT Devices and Sensors:

- **Function:** Gather current information on a range of factors, including energy usage, traffic volume, air quality, and structural integrity.
- **Example:** Energy-saving smart lighting with sensors in Barcelona, Spain, change brightness in response to pedestrian activity and outside factors.

#### 2.1.1.2. Machine Learning and Data Analytics:

- **Function:** Examine the information gathered in order to draw conclusions, identify patterns, and make wise choices.
- **Example:** The Hudson Yards in New York City monitor and optimize trash management, environmental conditions, and energy usage using a sophisticated data platform.

#### 2.1.1.3. Networks of Communication and Connectivity:

- **Function:** Guarantee smooth data transfer amongst stakeholders, systems, and devices.
- **Example:** The smart city program in Amsterdam depends on a strong fiber-optic network to link sensors and other equipment all around the city, allowing for real-time data management and exchange.

#### 2.1.1.4. Control and Automation Systems:

- **Function:** Put into practice automated reactions to data insights, including controlling energy loads or modifying traffic lights.
- **Example:** Singapore's smart traffic management system automatically modifies traffic lights based on real-time data to ease congestion and enhance traffic flow.

### 2.1.1.5. Platforms for Engagement and User Interfaces:

- **Function:** Give authorities and citizens access to data and command over infrastructure systems.
- **Example:** Dubliners can report problems, get information about public transit, and stay up to date on city services by using the MyDublin app.

### 2.1.1.6. Application of Smart Infrastructure

### 2.1.1.6.1. Smart Transportation:

- **Examples:**
- The Congestion Charge Zone in London monitors vehicle entry using cameras and sensors to ease traffic congestion.
- To enhance traffic flow, Los Angeles uses adaptive traffic signal control systems, which modify lights in response to real-time traffic data.

### 2.1.1.6.2. Smart Energy Grids:

- **Examples:**
- Include the Smart Grid Initiative in South Korea, which improves sustainability and efficiency by integrating renewable energy sources and enabling real-time energy management.
- The goal of Germany's Energiewende project is to manage energy supply and demand by integrating smart grid technologies and modernizing the energy system.

### 2.1.1.6.3. Smart Water Management:

- **Examples:**
- Singapore's water management system makes use of sensors to keep an eye on the flow and quality of the water, guaranteeing effective distribution and early leak identification.
- To maximize water use and minimize waste, Amsterdam uses predictive analytics and smart water meters.

### 2.1.1.6.4. Smart Buildings and Infrastructure:

- **Examples**:
- By modifying lighting and temperature according to occupancy and preferences, the Edge building in Amsterdam employs IoT and AI to provide a highly energy-efficient and user-friendly work environment.

- One World Trade Center in New York uses smart building technologies to improve security, comfort, and energy efficiency.

**2.1.1.6.5.    Waste Management:**

- **Examples:**
- To increase recycling rates and optimize waste collection routes, San Francisco's Recology program uses data analytics.
- By automating waste collection via a system of subterranean pneumatic tubes, Stockholm's Envac system improves cleanliness and efficiency.

**2.1.1.7.    The Advantages of Smart Infrastructure**

a. **Improved Efficiency:** Automation and real-time data cut waste and maximize resource usage.

b. **Better Quality of Life**: Smart systems improve waste management, energy, and transportation services.

c. **Sustainability**: By cutting emissions, preserving water, and incorporating renewable energy sources, smart infrastructure helps achieve environmental goals.

d. **Economic Development:** Attracting firms and investors is one way that smart infrastructure may promote economic growth.

e. **Resilience:** The capacity to respond to crises and natural disasters is enhanced by sophisticated monitoring and predictive analytics.

**2.1.1.8.    Challenges and Considerations:**

a. **Cost:** The adoption and upkeep of smart technologies need a substantial upfront cost.

b. **Privacy and Security:** Making sure that systems and data are shielded from online attacks.

c. **Interoperability:** It might be challenging to integrate various technologies and systems.

d. **Regulation and Governance:** Creating guidelines and structures to direct and control projects involving smart infrastructure.

In summary, by utilizing cutting-edge technologies to produce more effective, sustainable, and habitable settings, smart infrastructure represents a revolutionary approach to urban and rural development. Even though there are obstacles, the advantages and possibilities for improving life quality make this an enticing vision for the future.

## 2.2.  Urban Planning for the Future

Future urban planning entails conceiving and creating cities that are resilient, sustainable, and able to accommodate expanding populations. Innovative designs, cutting-edge technologies, and collaborative procedures are combined to create urban landscapes that improve quality of life while tackling issues like resource scarcity, population increase, and climate change.

### 2.2.1.  Important Guidelines for Future Urban Planning:

#### 2.2.1.1.  Sustainability:

- **Definition:** Planning cities to reduce their influence on the environment and to encourage the conservation of resources is defined.
- **Example:** Copenhagen wants to achieve carbon neutrality by 2025 by implementing sustainable urban planning strategies that include abundant bike lanes and green structures.

#### 2.2.1.2.  Resilience:

- **Definition:** Creating urban environments that are resilient to unfavorable occurrences like natural catastrophes and economic shocks.
- **Example:** The Resilient Neighborhoods initiative in New York City concentrates on community readiness and flood-resistant infrastructure to lessen the effects of climate change.

#### 2.1.1.3.  Integration of Technology with Smart Cities:

- **Definition:** Improving urban management and services through the application of technology like IoT, AI, and data analytics.
- **Example:** The Songdo International Business District in South Korea incorporates waste management technologies, smart grids, and networked buildings into its comprehensive plan to create a smart city.

#### 2.1.1.4.  Design Oriented on Humans:

- **Definition:** Giving inhabitants' wants and welfare top priority during urban planning processes.
- **Example:** Barcelona's Superblocks project rearranges city blocks to make urban areas more habitable by increasing green space, decreasing traffic, and improving air quality.

**2.1.1.5.    Mixed-Use Development:**

- **Definition:** Bringing together commercial, residential, and recreational areas to build thriving, walkable communities.
- **Example:** An illustration of a large-scale urban rehabilitation project that incorporates mixed-use developments to support a vibrant urban environment is the HafenCity project in Hamburg, Germany.

**2.1.1.6.    Participatory Planning:**

- **Definition:** Involving locals and interested parties in the planning process to guarantee inclusive and representative decision-making is the definition.
- **Example:** As an illustration, consider how the participatory planning approach has changed Medellín, Colombia, by incorporating locals in the creation of public areas and infrastructure initiatives.

**2.2.2.    New Developments in Urban Planning:**

**2.2.2.1.    Green and Blue Infrastructure:**

a. **Green Infrastructure:** Including parks, green roofs, and urban woods to create leisure areas and improve biodiversity.
   - **Example:** As an illustration, Singapore's Gardens by the Bay combines greenery with environmentally friendly architecture to enhance urban ecology and standard of living.

b. **Blue Infrastructure** refers to the management of water resources, such as lakes, wetlands, and rivers, with the goal of enhancing water quality and flood control.
   - **Example:** As an illustration, Rotterdam's Water Squares mix water management with public areas to collect extra rainfall and prevent flooding.

**2.2.2.2.    Transit Oriented Development (TOD):**

- **Definition:** Planning cities with effective public transportation networks in mind to lessen dependency on automobiles and encourage environmentally friendly mobility.
- **Example:** The Bus Rapid Transit (BRT) system in Curitiba, Brazil, is well known for guiding urban growth and easing traffic congestion.

**2.2.2.3.    Using the Circular Economy in Urban Design:**

- **Definition:** Putting into practice methods that help urban systems recycle resources, reuse materials, and reduce trash.

- **Example**: Amsterdam is leading the way in implementing circular economy concepts in urban planning, emphasizing waste minimization, sustainable building practices, and material reuse.

### 2.2.2.4. Inclusive and Cost-Effective Housing:

- **Definition:** Providing all socioeconomic groups with affordable housing options in order to advance social inclusion and equity.
- **Example**: The social housing concept in Vienna offers citizens high-quality, reasonably priced housing options while promoting social cohesion and diversity.

### 2.2.2.5. Smart Mobility Solutions:

- **Definition:** Using technology to enhance shared mobility services, electric and driverless vehicles, and other urban transportation systems.
- **Example:** To provide smooth and effective urban mobility, Helsinki's MaaS (Mobility as a Service) platform combines multiple transit choices into a single app.

### 2.2.2.6. Climate-Responsive Urban Planning:

- **Definition:** Developing urban areas with the ability to adjust and lessen the consequences of climate change, including increasing sea levels and temperatures.
- **Example**: The Climate Resilient Neighborhood project in Copenhagen uses permeable surfaces, green roofs, and raised structures as adaptable storm water management techniques.

### 2.2.3. Challenges in Future Urban Planning:

### 2.2.3.1. Finances & Economic Constraints:

- Large-scale urban projects can be difficult to finance, particularly in poor nations.
- **Example:** Financial and budgetary limitations frequently cause infrastructure projects in places like Mumbai to be delayed.

### 2.2.3.2. Integration of Policy and Governance:

- Although it is frequently difficult, coordination between various government agencies and levels is essential.
- **Example:** In large urban regions like Los Angeles, integrating land use policy and transportation planning involves substantial inter-agency collaboration.

### 2.2.3.3. Concerns About Technology and Data Privacy:

- Smart technologies have many advantages, but they also give rise to worries about cybersecurity and data privacy.
- **Example**: As an illustration, putting smart city concepts into practice in places like Toronto requires attending to citizens' worries about privacy and data usage.

**2.2.3.4.  Inclusion and Social Equity:**
- It can be quite difficult to guarantee that every resident benefits from urban advances, especially in varied communities.
- **Example**: Urban regeneration initiatives in places like New York must offer fair solutions while taking into account the relocation of low-income neighborhoods.

In summary, the goal of future urban planning is to integrate cutting-edge technologies, creative designs, and inclusive procedures to build livable, resilient, and sustainable cities. Through an emphasis on human-centered design, smart technology, sustainability, resilience, and participatory planning, urban planners may effectively tackle current issues and construct cities that cater to the requirements of coming generations. Examples from cities all over the world show how innovative urban planning has the power to change urban settings and raise everyone's standard of living.

## 2.3.  Building Resilient Cities

Creating metropolitan regions that are robust to a range of shocks and pressures, such as natural catastrophes, climate change, economic upheavals, and social issues, is the process of *Building Resilient Cities*. The goal of resilience in urban planning is to make cities more resilient to these shocks while preserving vital services and operations.

**2.3.1.  Important Elements of Urban Resilience**:

**2.3.1.1.  Infrastructure Resilience**:
- **Definition:** Ensuring the resilience and speedy recovery of physical infrastructure, including buildings, roads, bridges, and utilities, in the event of interruptions.
- **Example**: Tokyo, Japan, uses sophisticated seismic design methods together with building and infrastructure upgrades to lessen the effects of earthquakes.

**2.3.1.2.  Environmental Resilience:**

- **Definition:** Improving urban ecosystems' capacity to withstand and rebound from environmental shocks like extreme weather and climate change is its definition.
- **Example**: The MillionTreesNYC program in New York City grows trees all throughout the city to manage storm water, enhance air quality, and lessen the effects of heat islands.

2.3.1.3. **Economic Resilience:**

- **Definition:** Encouraging a varied and flexible economy that can endure economic downturns and bounce back swiftly is its definition.
- **Example:** To protect itself from the instability of the global economy, Singapore diversifies its economy across a number of industries, including manufacturing, technology, and finance.

2.3.1.4. **Social Resilience:**

- **Definition**: Increasing community cohesion and social networks to improve the ability of the group as a whole to respond to and recover from crises.
- **Example**: To promote social inclusion and community resilience, Medellín, Colombia, has made investments in social infrastructure, such as parks, libraries, and community centers.

2.3.1.5. **Resilience of Institutions and Governance:**

- **Definition:** Creating strong governance structures and institutions that are capable of handling crises and managing them well.
- **Example**: For instance, to manage flood risks and urban resilience, Rotterdam, Netherlands, has developed a thorough climate adaption policy and governance framework.

2.3.2. **Strategies for Developing Resilient Cities:**

2.3.2.1. **Risk Assessment and Planning:**

- **Definition:** Carefully evaluating risks in order to pinpoint weak points and make appropriate plans.
- **Example**: As an illustration, the Community Safety Element in San Francisco provides thorough risk assessments for fires, earthquakes, and other hazards, which direct emergency response and urban design.

2.3.2.2. **Data Analytics and Smart Technologies:**

- **Definition:** Monitoring urban systems, anticipating disturbances, and improving decision-making through the use of IoT, AI, and big data.

- **Example**: As an illustration, Barcelona's smart city platform combines information from many urban systems to maximize emergency, traffic, and pollution response times.

**2.3.2.3.  Adaptive and Sustainable Design:**
- **Definition:** Putting into practice design ideas that improve urban surroundings' sustainability and flexibility.
- **Example**: The Climate Resilient Neighborhoods in Copenhagen manage runoff and lower the danger of flooding by utilizing raised structures, permeable surfaces, and green roofs.

**2.3.2.4.  Public Participation and Instruction:**
- **Definition:** Teaching locals about readiness and response while involving them in resilience planning.
- **Example**: For instance, the NOLA Ready program in New Orleans uses workshops, drills, and instructional materials to engage neighborhood members in disaster preparedness.

**2.3.2.5.  Ecosystems-Based Approaches:**
- **Definition**: Making use of natural systems, like wetlands for flood protection, to improve urban resilience.
- **Example**: For instance, the restoration of Seoul, South Korea's Cheonggyecheon Stream turned a paved-over stream into an urban park that reduces floods and offers open space for recreation.

**2.3.3. Examples of Resilient City Initiatives:**

**2.3.3.1.  Japan's Tokyo: Earthquake Resistant**
- **Initiatives:** Prolonged public education programs, early warning systems, and sophisticated earthquake-resistant building methods.
- **Result:** Improved capacity to endure and recuperate from regular earthquake events.

**2.3.3.2.  Netherlands' Rotterdam: Flood Resilience**
- **Initiatives:** The city has put creative flood control measures into place, like green roofs, floating residences, and water plazas.
- **Result:** Enhanced flood resistance by utilizing both natural and man-made infrastructure.

**2.3.3.3.  US City of New York: Climate Resilience**

- **Initiatives:** The goals of the OneNYC and PlaNYC programs are to manage storm water better, create more green space, and lower greenhouse gas emissions.
- **Result:** Enhanced urban resilience to the effects of climate change, such as rising sea levels and extreme weather.

### 2.3.3.4. Singapore: Resilience in the Environment and Economy

- **Initiatives:** A diversified economy, strong social safety nets, and vast green spaces such as the floodplain-serving Bishan-Ang Mo Kio Park. **Result:** A more resilient urban environment through a balanced approach to environmental sustainability and economic growth.

### 2.3.3.5. Resilience of the Community and Society in Medellín, Colombia

- **Initiatives**: To increase accessibility and social cohesion, social urbanism initiatives are being built, such as parks, libraries, and the Metrocable system.
- **Result**: Reduction of crime rates, improvement of marginalized neighborhoods, and development of community resilience are the outcomes.

## 2.3.4. Challenges in Resilient City Development:

### 2.3.4.1. Financing and Investment:

- A challenge for many cities is the need for large initial investments in resilience initiatives.
- **Example:** For instance, designing all-encompassing flood defenses or seismically retrofitting structures may be too expensive for less wealthy cities.

### 2.3.4.2. Integration and Coordination:

- Coordination across different government agencies and sectors is necessary for effective resilience planning, although it can be challenging.
- **Example:** Integrating resilience measures into current urban planning frameworks frequently necessitates bridging agency silos and bureaucratic lethargy.

### 2.3.4.3. Community Participation:

- It can be difficult to ensure significant community involvement in resilience planning, especially in populated and diverse cities.

- **Example:** Targeted outreach and culturally appropriate methods are necessary to involve marginalized communities in resilience programs.

**2.3.4.4. Data and Technology Challenges:**
- Technology provides answers, but it also raises issues with cybersecurity, data privacy, and equal access.
- **Example: S**trong data governance structures are necessary for smart city technology to handle privacy issues and guarantee inclusion.

In summary, the process of creating resilient cities is complex and requires combining social cohesiveness, economic diversity, environmental sustainability, and strong governance with resilient infrastructure. Urban planners may improve cities' ability to endure and recover from a variety of shocks and stressors by implementing comprehensive policies and taking inspiration from around the world. Notwithstanding obstacles, achieving urban resilience is essential to building livable, flexible, and sustainable cities in the future.

# Chapter 3: Internet of Things (IoT) in Smart Cities

## 3.1. Introduction to IoT

A network of networked devices that communicate and share data with one another over the internet is referred to as the *Internet of Things* (IoT). These gadgets gather and transfer data thanks to sensors, software, and other technologies built right into them. This allows for automation and intelligent decision-making in a variety of fields.

### 3.1.1. Important Parts of IoT:

### 3.1.1.1.  Devices and Sensors:

- **Function:** Gather environmental data, including location, motion, temperature, and humidity.
- **Example:** Temperature sensors are used by smart thermostats, such as the Nest Learning Thermostat, to maximize heating and cooling in houses.

### 3.1.1.2.  Connectivity:

- **Function:** Send data gathered by devices to central systems or other devices.
- **Examples** of networks that allow device communication and data sharing include Wi-Fi, Bluetooth, Zigbee, and cellular networks.

### 3.1.1.3.  Data Processing:

- **Function:** Examine the gathered information to obtain insightful understandings.
- **Example:** Big data processing from IoT devices is handled by cloud computing platforms like AWS IoT, which offers real-time analytics and machine learning capabilities.

### 3.1.1.4.  User Interfaces:

- **Function:** Give consumers the ability to examine data, control devices, and communicate with IoT systems.
- **Example:** Smartphone apps for smart home systems let users remotely monitor and manage household appliances.

### 3.1.1.5.  Actuators:

- **Function:** Take decisions and take action based on facts.
- **Example:** Smart locks can open doors on their own when a designated person gets close.

### 3.1.2. Applications of IoT:

The next stage of the industrial revolution is called the *Internet of Things* (IoT). Technology makes it possible to bring tangible objects into the digital sphere. The Internet of Things (IoT) is the merging of the "real world" with the "digital world," facilitating simple communication between individuals, things, and procedures.

The Internet of Things opens up possibilities for safe integration between computer systems and the physical world by enabling products to be activated and controlled remotely over an internet network infrastructure. In the actual world, IoT applications are altering how we carry out every social function. Science fiction no longer applies to IoT.

Connectivity to the internet has more power than just computers and cellphones. Physical devices can now record, monitor, and communicate data with minimal human intervention thanks to the internet. We'll look at the top internet of things (IoT) apps that are transforming various workplaces, homes, and industries.

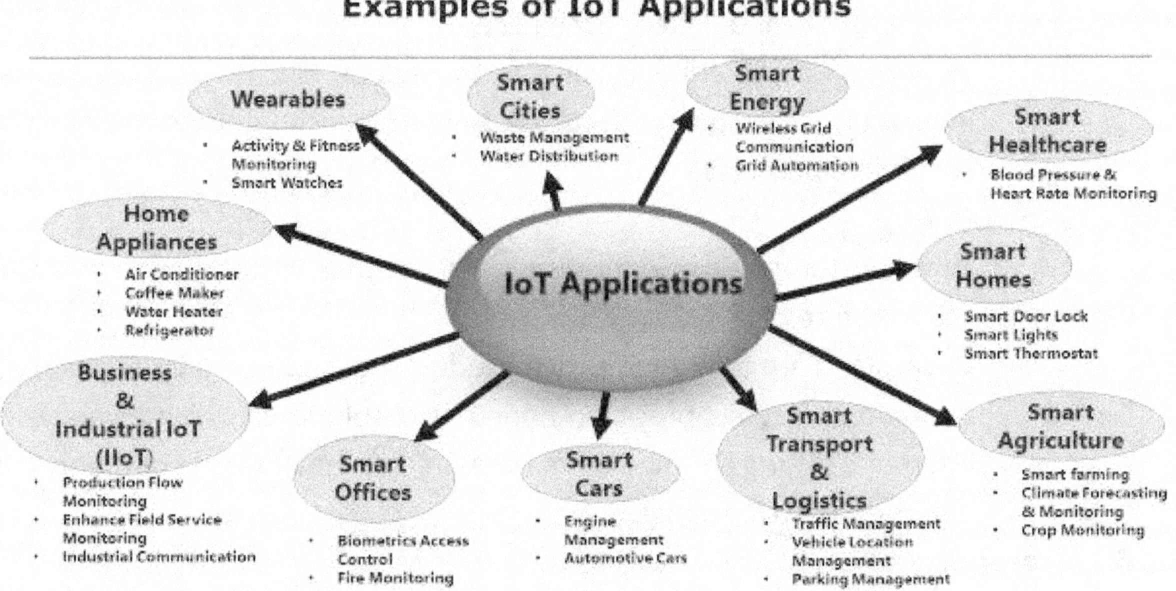


**Source:** Smart Cities: *The Technology Transforming Urban Living*, GoodMan Series, (Patrick Mukosha, 2024).

*Figure 3: Examples of IoT Applications*

### 3.1.2.1.  Smart Homes:

- **Devices:** home assistants, security cameras, lighting controls, and smart thermostats.

  **Example:** Customers can use voice commands or smartphone apps to manage lighting, security, and appliances by integrating multiple smart home devices with Amazon Echo and Google Nest Hub.

### 3.1.2.2.  Smart Cities:

- **Devices:** Air quality monitors, waste management systems, traffic sensors, and smart streetlights.

- **Example:** Barcelona employs IoT to control street lighting, lowering energy use by modifying light intensity in response to real-time information on vehicle and pedestrian traffic.

### 3.1.2.3. Medical Care:

- **Devices:** Smart medical devices, wearable health monitors, and remote patient monitoring systems.
- **Example:** By providing patients and healthcare professionals with real-time blood sugar levels, continuous glucose monitors (CGMs) like those made by Dexcom help to better control diabetes.

### 3.1.2.4. Industrial (IIoT):

- **Devices** include automation systems, sensors for predictive maintenance, and linked machinery.
- **Example:** The Predix platform from General Electric uses IoT to track industrial machinery, forecast maintenance requirements, and streamline processes.

### 3.1.2.5. Agriculture:

- **Devices:** automatic irrigation systems, weather stations, and sensors for soil moisture.
- **Example:** Farmers can improve productivity and resource efficiency by using John Deere's precision agricultural solutions, which leverage the Internet of Things to give them data on crop health, soil conditions, and equipment performance.

### 3.1.2.6. Transportation:

- **Devices:** Include fleet tracking, traffic management systems, and connected cars.
- **Example:** To enable semi-autonomous driving, for instance, Tesla's Autopilot function leverages the Internet of Things to gather data from sensors and cameras in order to navigate and avoid hazards.

### 3.1.3. Benefits of IoT:

### 3.1.3.1. Enhanced Productivity

- Real-time monitoring and automation maximize resource utilization while reducing waste.
- **Example:** Smart grids dynamically balance the supply and demand for electricity, minimizing waste and boosting dependability.

### 3.1.3.2. Improved Standard of Living:

- Convenience, safety, and health outcomes are all enhanced by IoT solutions in healthcare, home automation, and urban management.
- **Example:** Wearable fitness trackers assist users in tracking their health and fitness objectives.

### 3.1.3.3. Savings On Costs:

- Numerous sectors see reduced operating expenses as a result of predictive maintenance and enhanced operations.
- **Example:** In the manufacturing industry, IoT-enabled predictive maintenance helps avert expensive equipment breakdowns and downtime.

### 3.1.3.4. Making Decisions Based on Data: (Data-Driven Decision Making)

- Informed decision-making across sectors is supported by real-time data collection and analysis.
- **Example:** Retailers can more efficiently manage inventories and provide individualized consumer experiences by utilizing IoT data.

### 3.1.4. IoT Challenges:

### 3.1.4.1. Security and Privacy:

- Because IoT devices gather and send sensitive data, it is imperative to ensure data security and user privacy.
- **Example:** In 2016, the Mirai botnet assault took advantage of weak IoT devices, emphasizing the necessity for strong security protocols.

### 3.1.4.2. Interoperability:

- It can be difficult to integrate disparate IoT systems and devices from various manufacturers.
- **Example:** There could not be smooth connectivity and various apps needed for smart home devices from different brands.

### 3.1.4.3. Scalability:

- It can be difficult to manage and analyze massive volumes of data from millions of devices on current infrastructure.
- **Example:** Internet of Things platforms must expand well to accommodate the increasing volumes of data and linked devices.

### 3.1.4.4. Energy Consumption:

- Since many Internet of Things (IoT) devices run on batteries, energy-efficient designs are necessary to extend battery life.

- **Example:** In order to reduce maintenance, IoT sensors in isolated or difficult-to-reach areas need long-lasting power supplies.

In summary, the Internet of Things (IoT) is a *game-changing technology that links systems and devices to allow for automation and intelligent decision-making in a variety of fields.* Smart cities and homes, as well as healthcare and business uses, all benefit from the Internet of Things' ability to increase productivity, improve quality of life, and offer insightful data. To fully achieve the potential, though, issues with security, interoperability, scalability, and energy consumption need to be resolved. IoT will remain crucial in influencing linked living and intelligent systems in the future as technology develops.

## 3.2. IoT Applications in Urban Management

The Internet of Things (IoT) is bringing real-time data, efficiency gains, and improved urban quality of life together to transform urban management. *Through the incorporation of IoT technologies into several facets of urban infrastructure, cities can attain increased intelligence, sustainability, and resilience.*

### 3.2.1. Important Areas of IoT Applications in Urban Management:

#### 3.2.1.1. Smart Transportation Systems:

a. **Traffic Management:**
   - o **Example:** *Los Angeles* has an innovative system that employs cameras and Internet of Things sensors to monitor traffic flow and modify traffic signals in real-time, lowering traffic and speeding up travel times.

b. **Public Transit Optimization:**
   - o **Example:** To improve commuter comfort and system efficiency, *Singapore's public transportation system* leverages the Internet of Things (IoT) to deliver real-time updates on bus and train locations, schedules, and passenger loads.

c. **Parking Management:**
   - o **Example:** *Barcelona* has installed smart parking systems that use sensors to identify open spots and give drivers real-time information through a smartphone app, cutting down on the amount of time spent looking for parking and easing traffic congestion.

**3.2.1.2.  Energy Management:**
  a.  **Smart Grids:**
      o **Example:**  One example is the *Pecan Street Project in Austin*, Texas, which combines sensors and IoT-enabled smart meters to optimize energy distribution and minimize outages by monitoring and controlling electrical demand.
  b.  **Street Lighting:**
      o **Example:**  *Copenhagen* has deployed smart streetlights with Internet of Things sensors that modify illumination intensity in response to car and pedestrian movement. This reduces energy usage and maintenance expenses dramatically.

**3.2.1.3.  Management of Waste:**
  a.  **Smart Waste Bins:**
      o **Example:**  In *Seoul, South Korea*, sensors-equipped IoT-enabled rubbish bins keep an eye on fill levels and optimize waste collection routes to cut down on operating expenses and the environmental effect.
  b.  **Recycling Programs:**
      o **Example:**  *San Francisco's* waste management system tracks recycling rates and offers data-driven insights to enhance the efficiency of waste segregation and recycling.

**3.2.1.4.  Water Resources Management:**
  a.  **Smart Water Meters:**
      o **Example:**  In *Singapore*, these meters offer real-time information on water consumption, which aids in leak detection, waste reduction, and the promotion of water efficiency.
  b.  **Flood Management:**
      o **Example:**  *Rotterdam's intelligent flood control system* employs Internet of Things sensors to track water levels and regulate storm water pumps and barriers, therefore reducing the likelihood of flooding and safeguarding city infrastructure.

**3.2.1.5.  Environmental Surveillance:**
  a.  **Air Quality Monitoring:**
      o **Example:** A network of Internet of Things (IoT) sensors monitors *air pollution levels in London*, giving citizens access to real-time

information through a smartphone app and data to support public health initiatives.

### b. Monitoring of Noise Pollution:

- o **Example:** *New York City* employs Internet of Things (IoT)-enabled sound sensors to track noise levels throughout various neighborhoods, assisting in the enforcement of noise laws and enhancing urban living standards.

**3.2.1.6. Security and Safety for the Public:**

### a. Surveillance Systems:

- o **Example:** *Chicago*'s smart surveillance network monitors high-crime areas by integrating IoT cameras and sensors, allowing for real-time alerts and quicker law enforcement reaction times.

### b. Disaster Response:

- o **Example:** *Tokyo* employs Internet of Things (IoT) sensors to identify seismic activity and send out early earthquake alerts, enabling prompt evacuation and the implementation of disaster preparedness procedures.

**3.2.1.7. Building Management:**

### a. Smart Buildings:

- o **Example:** The *Edge Building* in Amsterdam uses Internet of Things (IoT) to monitor and control energy use, lighting, heating, and ventilation, resulting in a very comfortable and productive work environment.

### b. Maintenance and Operations:

- o **Example:** IoT sensors in Dubai's buildings track structural health and maintenance requirements, anticipating problems before they get out of hand and guaranteeing peak building efficiency.

**3.2.1.8. Citizen Engagement:**

### a. Smart City Platforms:

- o **Example:** The *MyHelsinki platform* in Helsinki enables locals to report problems, obtain up-to-date information about city services, and take part in the planning process, all of which promote increased openness and community involvement.

### b. E-Government Services:

  o **Example:** *Tallinn, Estonia*, enhances civic engagement and administrative efficiency by offering a broad range of e-government services, such as voting and public service requests, by utilizing IoT and digital platforms.

## 3.2.2. IoT's Advantages in Urban Management:

### 3.2.2.1. Increased Efficiency:

- Urban management procedures are streamlined by IoT, which lowers operating expenses and resource consumption.
- **Example:** Smart grids optimize power distribution and cut down on energy waste, which lowers utility costs and boosts service dependability.

### 3.2.2.2. Enhanced Quality of Life:

- IoT applications improve urban infrastructure and public services, which benefits people' quality of life.
- **Example:** Homeowners can take preventative measures during times of high pollution thanks to real-time air quality monitoring, which improves health outcomes.

### 3.2.2.3. Sustainability:

- Through effective resource management and environmentally friendly practices, IoT assists cities in lessening their environmental impact.
- **Examples** of sustainable urban living include smart water meters and waste management systems, which lower waste and encourage conservation.

### 3.2.2.4. Enhanced Security and Safety:

- Through enhanced emergency management, disaster response, and surveillance systems, IoT improves public safety.
- **Example:** Early warning systems for natural catastrophes facilitate prompt evacuations and lessen the effect of crises on populated cities.

### 3.2.2.5. Data-based Decision Making:

- IoT device real-time data offers insightful information for policy and urban development.
- **Example:** Better road networks and public transportation systems are designed by city planners with the use of data from smart traffic systems, which eases traffic and increases mobility.

## 3.2.3. Challenges in IoT Implementation in Urban Management:

### 3.2.3.1. Data Security and Privacy

- It is essential to safeguard the enormous volumes of data gathered by IoT devices in order to stop breaches and abuse.
- **Example:** Making sure that the infrastructure of smart cities has strong cybersecurity safeguards in place to fend off cyberattacks.

### 3.2.3.2. Interoperability:

- It can be difficult to integrate different IoT systems and devices from different manufacturers.
- **Example:** Develop uniform standards and protocols to guarantee smooth communication amongst various IoT devices.

### 3.2.3.3. Infrastructure and Cost:

- IoT infrastructure can have substantial upfront costs as well as continuous maintenance costs.
- **Example:** Showing long-term benefit and balancing implementation costs of smart city technologies with financial limits.

### 3.2.3.4. Complexity of Technology:

- High-tech capabilities are needed to manage and analyze massive amounts of data from IoT devices.
- **Example:** Constructing strong data analytics systems to handle and analyze information from several Internet of Things sensors is one example.

### 3.2.3.5. Community Acceptance:

- Achieving public acceptability and trust is crucial for the effective use of IoT technologies.
- **Example:** Involve locals in the development and implementation of IoT initiatives to allay worries and emphasize advantages.

In summary, urban management IoT applications have the revolutionary potential to build smarter, more sustainable cities. Cities may boost public services, raise living standards, and increase resilience by incorporating IoT technologies into numerous facets of their infrastructure. Smart cities of the future are made possible by the enormous benefits of IoT in urban administration, despite obstacles pertaining to data privacy, interoperability, cost, and community acceptance.

# Chapter 4: Harnessing Big Data and Analytics

## 4.1. Understanding Big Data

Big data is the term used to describe *data sets that are too big or complicated for conventional data-processing application software to handle.* While data with more features or columns and higher complexity may result in a higher false discovery rate, data with many entries (rows) give greater statistical power. The best interpretation is that *it is a vast body of information that cannot be understood when used sparingly, even though it is occasionally used loosely due to a lack of official definition.*

Data collection, data storage, data analysis, search, sharing, transfer, visualization, querying, updating, information privacy, and data source are some of the problems associated with *Big Data Analysis*. Three fundamental ideas were initially connected to big data: volume, variety, and velocity. Big data analysis makes sampling difficult, which previously limited the options to observations and sample. Thus, the quality or perceptiveness of the data is referred to as a fourth term, truthfulness. The volume and variety of data might result in expenses and hazards that surpass an organization's ability to generate and extract value from big data if insufficient investment in expertise for big data veracity is made.

Thus, the term "*Big Data*" describes the *enormous amounts of data that are produced quickly from a range of sources, such as social media, sensors, transactions, and more*. The three Vs: volume, velocity, and variety, define it. Comprehending Big Data entails knowing its properties, the technology that handle and examine it, and the various industries in which it is applied.

### 4.1.1. Characteristics of Big Data:

#### 4.1.1.1. Volume:

- **Definition:** The massive volume of data produced per second.
- **Example:** For instance, every day, social networking sites like Facebook produce terabytes of user data, including multimedia material, likes, comments, and posts.

#### 4.1.1.2. Velocity:

- **Definition:** The rate at which information is created and analyzed.
- **Example:** For instance, in order to make wise decisions, financial markets produce enormous volumes of real-time trade data that must be processed almost instantly.

#### 4.1.1.3. Variety:

- **Definition:** The many forms of data, both organized and unorganized, are defined.
- **Example:** Big Data includes information from transaction records, social media posts, emails, videos, and sensor data, among other sources.

#### 4.1.1.4. Veracity:

- **Definition:** The data's accuracy and dependability.

- **Example:** In the healthcare industry, where inaccurate data might result in misdiagnoses or treatment plans, it is imperative to ensure data quality and accuracy.

4.1.1.5. **Value:**

- **Definition:** The data's value in producing insights that can be put into practice.
- **Example:** Retailers, for instance, use consumer purchase information to better understand purchasing trends and enhance inventory control.

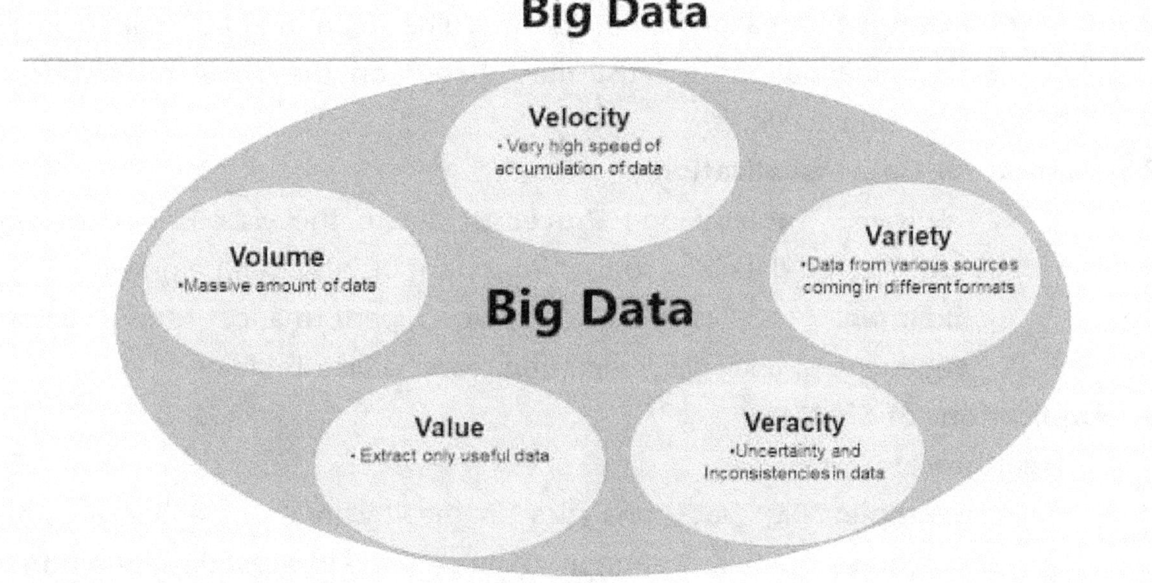


**Source:** Smart Cities: *The Technology Transforming Urban Living*; GoodMan Series, (Patrick Mukosha, 2024).

*Figure 4: Big Data - Characteristics*

## 4.1.2. **Technologies for Big Data Processing**:

4.1.2.1. **Data Storage Solutions:**

- **Hadoop** is an open-source platform that enables massive data volumes to be processed across computer clusters in a distributed manner.
- **Example:** Hadoop is used by businesses like Yahoo and Facebook to handle and process their enormous volumes of data.

4.1.2.2. **Frameworks for Data Processing:**

- **Apache Spark:** a well-known, quick, and user-friendly open-source unified analytics engine for big data processing.

- **Example:** Financial institutions employ Apache Spark for fraud detection and real-time analytics.

4.1.2.3. **Platforms for Data Management:**

- **NoSQL Databases**: These are scalable, unstructured data-handling databases, such as MongoDB, Cassandra, and HBase.
- **Example**: Netflix manages massive volumes of user data and guarantees high availability using Cassandra.

4.1.2.4. **Tools for Data Analytics:**

- **AI and Machine Learning:** These are fields that utilize models and algorithms to evaluate and forecast vast amounts of data.
- **Example:** Amazon employs machine learning to make product recommendations to customers based on their past purchases and browsing activities.

4.1.2.5. **Tools for Data Visualization:**

- Tools like **Tableau** and **Power BI** aid in the visualization of large, complicated data sets so that important insights can be drawn.
- **Example:** To visualize campaign performance and customer engagement analytics, marketing teams utilize Tableau.

4.1.3. **Applications of Big Data:**

4.1.3.1. **Healthcare:**

- **Example:** Big data analytics in healthcare can enhance patient outcomes, optimize treatment regimens, and forecast disease outbreaks. For example, IBM Watson Health analyzes medical literature and patient information using Big Data to help diagnose and prescribe treatments for cancer patients.

4.1.3.2. **Retail:**

- **Example:** Walmart examines enormous volumes of transaction data to manage supply chains, improve inventories, and provide customers with a customized shopping experience. This enhances consumer happiness and lowers stock outs.

4.1.3.3. **Finance:**

- **Example:** Risk management, fraud detection, and customized financial services are all made possible by the use of big data in finance. Credit card issuers, for example, utilize real-time data analytics to identify fraudulent transactions and stop losses.

4.1.3.4. **Urban Planning:**
- **Example:** Cities employ big data to better control traffic, upgrade urban infrastructure, and improve public transportation. For example, the City of Chicago predicts traffic congestion and optimizes public transit routes using data from multiple sensors and sources.

4.1.3.5. **Marketing:**
- **Example:** For instance, Procter & Gamble and other businesses use big data to segment markets, study consumer behavior, and develop customized marketing plans. This makes it possible to target audiences more precisely and increase marketing campaigns' return on investment (ROI).

4.1.3.6. **Energy:**
- **Example:** Utility firms use big data to integrate renewable energy sources, forecast trends of energy demand, and manage power grids. Smart grids balance supply and demand by utilizing real-time data, which lowers energy waste and boosts efficiency.

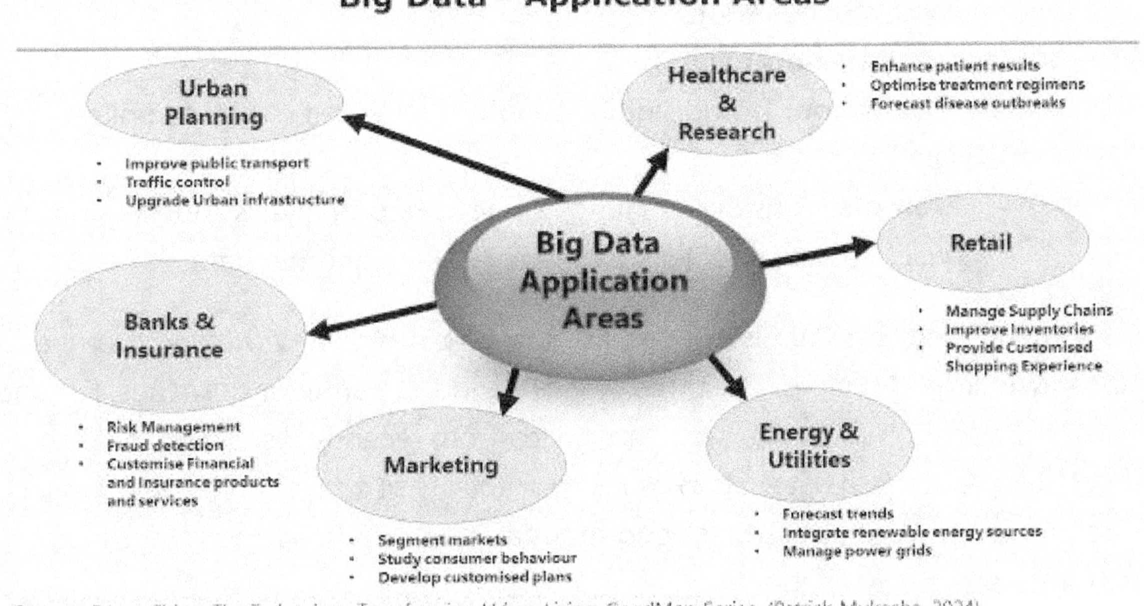


**Source:** Smart Cities: *The Technology Transforming Urban Living*, GoodMan Series, (Patrick Mukosha, 2024).

*Figure 5: Big Data - Application Areas*

## 4.1.4. Big Data's Challenges

### 4.1.4.1. Data Security and Privacy:

- **Description:** Preserving confidential data against security breaches and guaranteeing adherence to laws such as GDPR.
- **Example:** Making sure that, in order to avoid unwanted access, client data gathered by online services is encrypted and access-controlled.

### 4.1.4.2. Data Quality:

- **Description:** Guaranteeing the precision, completeness, and dependability of information.
- **Example:** Cleanse and verify data from several sources before analysis to prevent false conclusions.

### 4.1.4.3. Scalability:

- **Description:** Effectively managing the growing amount and intricacy of information.
- **Example:** consider using cloud computing or other scalable storage methods to manage expanding data sets.

### 4.1.4.4. Integration:

- **Description:** Integrating information from various systems and sources.
- **Example:** combining information from social media, e-commerce sites, and CRM systems to obtain a comprehensive understanding of consumer behavior.

### 4.1.4.5. Interpretation and Analysis:

- **Description:** Taking significant information out of big, complicated data sets.
- **Example:** consider creating sophisticated analytics models and hiring qualified data scientists to reliably understand big data.

As earlier mentioned, Big data is defined as data with a higher *Variety* that arrives at a *Velocity* and in larger *Volumes*. The three "Vs" are another name for this. Thus, Big data is simply larger, more complex data sets, particularly from recently discovered data sources. The sheer volume of these data sets exceeds the capacity of conventional data processing software. However, you may use these enormous amounts of data to solve business issues that you were previously unable to.

In summary, gaining an understanding of big data is essential to utilizing its potential to spur innovation, productivity, and decision-making in a variety of industries. *Organizations may use Big Data to obtain insightful information, enhance operations, and provide better services by implementing the appropriate technology and tackling the related difficulties*. Whether applied strategically, big data is changing industries and influencing the direction of business and technology, whether in healthcare, retail, finance, energy, or urban planning.

## 4.2. Data Sources and Collection Methods for Big Data

The methodical process of obtaining measurements or observations is known as *Data Collection*. Gaining first-hand knowledge and unique insights into your study challenge is made possible through data collecting, regardless of whether you are conducting research for academic, governmental, or business goals.

Although the goals and techniques used in different sectors may vary, the general data collection procedure is still very much the same. Prior to starting the data collection process, take into account:

- The purpose of the study or research;
- The kind of data you plan to collect;
- The techniques and protocols you'll employ to gather, store, and handle the data.

Use these four procedures to gather high-quality data that is pertinent to your goals.

- **Step 1:** Clearly state the purpose of your study;
- **Step 2:** Select the mode of data collecting;
- **Step 3:** Make a plan for collecting data.;
- **Step 4:** Collect Data.

Let's examine each of these steps a little more:
- **Step 1:**
    - Clearly define your research's objectives before beginning the data collection process. You can do this by first creating a problem statement, which asks what is the practical or scientific issue you want to address and why it matters.
    - Next, you should develop one or more research questions that specifically state what you want to learn. Depending on your research questions, you may need to gather. Statistical techniques are used to analyze quantitative data, which is represented by numbers and graphs.

Words are used to describe qualitative data, which is then interpreted and categorized for analysis.

- o Gather quantitative data if your goal is to verify a theory, measure something exactly, or obtain extensive statistical insights. Gather qualitative data if your goal is to investigate concepts, comprehend experiences, or obtain in-depth understanding of a particular situation.
- o You can utilize a mixed methods strategy, which gathers both kinds of data, if you have multiple goals.

- **Step 2:**
  - o Select the mode of data collecting
  - o Select the approach that will work best for your research based on the data you hope to gather. The primary method used in experimental research is quantitative.
  - o Qualitative approaches include ethnographies, focus groups, and interviews.
  - o Secondary data gathering, observations, surveys, and archive research can all be done using quantitative or qualitative techniques.
  - o Take great care when deciding on the data collection strategy that will enable you to directly address your research objectives.

- **Step 3:**
  - o Make a plan for gathering data.
  - o Once you have decided which approach or methods to use, you must precisely determine how you will put them into practice.
  - o What steps will you take to ensure that the variables you are interested in are accurately observed or measured? For example, choose the format of the questions if you're doing surveys or interviews, and choose the experimental design if you're conducting an experiment.

- **Step 4:**
  - o Collect Data - as desired.

Comprehending Big Data entails not only the technologies utilized for data processing and analysis, but also the sources and techniques used for data collection. Gathering data in an efficient manner is essential to producing trustworthy and useful insights.

4.2.1. **Primary Data Sources:**

4.2.1.1. **Social Media:**

- **Platforms:** LinkedIn, Instagram, Facebook, Twitter, and so forth. User posts, comments, likes, shares, and multimedia content are all collected as data.
- **Method of Collection:** Web scraping, third-party data aggregators, and APIs offered by social media networks.
- **Example:** Consider social media sentiment analysis for brand management, in which businesses track brand mentions to determine how the public feels about them.

4.2.1.2. **Sensor Data:**

- **Devices:** These include wearable technology, smart meters, ambient sensors, and Internet of Things gadgets.
- **Data Collected:** Temperature, humidity, motion, air quality, health metrics, and energy use are among the data gathered.
- **Method of Collection:** Direct data transfer via networks (Wi-Fi, cellular, Bluetooth, Zigbee) from sensors to central databases.
- **Example:** Real-time traffic and air quality monitoring is possible in smart cities thanks to IoT sensors.

4.2.1.3. **Transaction Data:**

- **Sources:** Online transactions, financial systems, and point-of-sale systems are the sources.
- **Data Collected:** Purchase information, payment methods, transaction amounts, and timestamps are among the data gathered.
- **Method of Collection:** automated data collection via e-commerce platforms and connected transaction systems.
- **Example:** Retailers, for instance, examine transaction data to better understand consumer behavior and streamline inventory control.

4.2.1.4. **Web Data:**

- **Sources:** Digital platforms, websites, and online services are sources.
- **Data Collected:** User activity logs, clickstreams, browsing histories, and form submissions are among the data gathered.
- **Collection Methods:** Cookies, tracking pixels, and web analytics tools are the methods of collection.
- **Example:** Web analytics, for instance, are used by e-commerce websites to monitor user activity and customize the buying experience.

4.2.1.5. **Machine-Generated Data:**

- **Sources:** Automated systems, servers, network records, and industrial equipment.
- **Data Collected:** Operational logs, error logs, performance measurements, and system alarms are among the data gathered.
- **Method of Collection:** Network management systems, log files, and system monitoring tools.
- **Example:** IT departments track network performance and look for irregularities using machine-generated data.

4.2.1.6. **Public Data:**

- **Sources** include open data platforms, public documents, and government databases.
- **Data Collected:** Health statistics, economic indicators, environmental data, and demographic data.
- **Method of Collection:** Downloading data via public data platforms' APIs and official websites.
- **Example:** For example, to create more efficient city layouts, urban planners use publicly available data on traffic and population density.

4.2.1.7. **Business Systems:**

- **Sources:** enterprise software such as HR, ERP, and CRM systems.
- **Data Collected:** Financial information, personnel files, sales information, and customer interactions.
- **Method of Collection:** Integration via database connectors and APIs with enterprise applications is the method of collection.
- **Example:** For instance, businesses examine CRM data to enhance sales and customer relationship management tactics.

4.2.2. **Techniques for Data Collection:**

4.2.2.1. **Applications Programming Interfaces (APIs):**

- **Function:** Facilitate data sharing and communication across apps.
- **Use Case:** Gathering information from banking services, social media sites, and other websites.
- **Example:** The Twitter API makes it possible to get user interaction data and tweets for sentiment analysis.

4.2.2.2. **Web Scraping:**

- **Function:** Automated scripts that extract data from websites.

- **Use Case:** Data collection from news websites, e-commerce sites, and public websites.
- **Example:** Gathering feedback and emotion from customers by scraping product reviews from e-commerce websites.

4.2.2.3. **Gathering Data via Streaming:**
- **Function:** Real-time data processing and acquisition as it is produced.
- **Use Case:** Keeping an eye on social media streams, financial market data, and real-time feeds from IoT devices.
- **Example:** Financial institutions employ streaming data to instantly execute deals and assess stock market movements.

4.2.2.4. **Data Lakes:**
- **Function:** The purpose of centralized repositories is to hold unprocessed data in its original format until required.
- **Use Case:** Keeping a lot of data, both organized and unorganized, from various sources.
- **Example:** For thorough analysis, a retail corporation stores transactional data, customer data, and web logs in a data lake.

4.2.2.5. **Log Files:**
- **Function:** Keeping track of system transactions and occurrences.
- **Use Case:** Tracking application usage, security events, and system performance.
- **Example:** To monitor system health and address issues, an IT team employs server log files.

4.2.2.6. **Questionnaires & Surveys:**
- **Function:** Directly gathering personal information from people.
- **Use Case:** Compiling data from market research, employee satisfaction surveys, and consumer feedback.
- **Example:** Businesses poll customers to get their opinions on their goods and services.

4.2.2.7. **Manual Data Entry:**
- **Function:** Manually entering data into systems.
- **Use Case:** Gathering information about specialized industries or handwritten forms that cannot be automatically generated.
- **Example:** Healthcare professionals manually input patient data into electronic health record (EHR) systems.

4.2.3. **Examples of Big Data Collection in Projects:**

4.2.3.1. **Smart City Projects:**
- **City:** Spain's *Barcelona*
- **Data Sources**: Internet of Things sensors monitoring energy use, trash management, traffic flow, and air quality.
- **Data Collection Methods:** Sensors transmit data in real time to centralized city management platforms.
- **Result:** Better public services, less energy use, and better urban planning.

4.2.3.2. **Retail Analytics:**
- **Organization:** *Walmart*
- **Data Sources:** Point-of-sale systems, internet transactions, and consumer loyalty programs are examples of data sources.
- **Collection Methods:** Web analytics tools and automated transaction capture are the two methods of collection.
- **Results:** Personalized marketing, better inventory management, and enhanced customer satisfaction are the results.

4.2.3.3. **Perspectives on Healthcare:**
- **Establishment:** *IBM Watson Well-being*
- **Information Sources:** Genomic data, clinical trial data, and medical records.
- **Methods of Collection:** Real-time data access through APIs and integration with healthcare databases.
- **Results:** Personalized treatment strategies, better illness diagnosis, and better patient outcomes are the results.

4.2.3.4. **Analysis of Financial Markets:**
- **Organization:** *JPMorgan Chase*
- **Data sources** include transaction records, economic statistics, and stock market data.
- **Data Gathering Techniques** include APIs from financial data suppliers and streaming data collection.
- **Result:** Fraud detection, risk management, and real-time trading techniques.

In summary, Big Data is gathered using a variety of techniques, each specifically designed to meet the requirements of the data being gathered, and from a broad range of sources. The sources are numerous and ever-expanding, ranging from public data and transaction records to social media and sensors. Organizations can leverage the power of Big Data by utilizing efficient data collecting techniques like web scraping, APIs, streaming data collection, and data lakes. Organizations can better manage and analyze their data to support insights and decision-making across a variety of sectors by being aware of these sources and techniques.

## 4.3. Transforming Data into Insights

Data collection, processing, analysis, and visualization are some of the crucial processes involved in turning data into insights that can be put into practice. Organizations can use this technique to use Big Data for strategic planning and well-informed decision-making. We will go over each of these processes in more detail below, along with some instances of how various industries have accomplished this change.

### 4.3.1. Procedures for Converting Data into Insights

#### 4.3.1.1. Data Collection:

- **Description:** The process of collecting unprocessed data from several platforms, including public databases, social media, transactional systems, and sensors.
- **Example:** Retailers, for instance, get information from online transactions, consumer feedback forms, and point-of-sale systems.

#### 4.3.1.2. Processing Data:

- **Description:** Data organization, transformation, and cleaning are done to prepare it for analysis. This covers resolving missing values, eliminating duplicates, and standardizing formats.
- **Example**: When processing patient records, a healthcare provider makes sure that medical terminology and forms are consistent.

#### 4.3.1.3. Storage of Data:

- **Description:** Keeping processed data available for analysis by storing it in databases, data warehouses, or data lakes.
- **Example:** For instance, data warehouses are used by financial firms to effectively and safely store transaction data.

#### 4.3.1.4. Analyzing Data:

- **Description:** To find patterns, trends, and correlations in the data, statistical approaches, machine learning algorithms, and data mining techniques are applied.
- **Example:** Marketing departments can forecast consumer behavior using predictive analytics by using historical purchase data.

4.3.1.5. **Data Visualization:**

- **Description:** Making data insights understandable and useful by presenting them in visual representations like dashboards, graphs, and charts.
- **Example:** The transportation department of a city employs dashboards to show congestion hotspots and real-time traffic statistics.

4.3.1.6. **Creating Insights:**

- **Description:** Applying analytical data interpretation to produce practical insights that guide decision-making.
- **Example:** To enhance user experience and optimize website layout, an e-commerce company leverages insights from web analytics.

4.3.1.7. **Making Decisions:**

- **Description:** Utilizing the knowledge acquired to guide well-informed decisions that support operational enhancements and corporate strategy.
- **Example:** To minimize downtime, a manufacturer schedules proactive equipment repairs using information from predictive maintenance.

4.3.2. **Examples of Data Transformation into Insights:**

4.3.2.1. **Retail Industry:**

- **Organization**: *Amazon*
- **Data Collection**: Product reviews, surfing habits, and purchase histories of customers are all sources of data.
- **Data processing** involves combining and cleansing information from several sources.
- **Data Storage:** Scalable data storage can be achieved by data lakes and warehouses.
- **Data Analysis:** Algorithms for machine learning in recommendation systems.
- **Data Visualisation:** Dashboards displaying consumer preferences and sales patterns are examples of data visualization.

- **Insight Generation:** Personalized product suggestions and focused marketing initiatives are examples of insight generation.
- **Results:** The result is better consumer satisfaction and higher revenue thanks to customized shopping experiences.

4.3.2.2. **Healthcare Industry:**

- **Establishment:** *Mayo Clinic*
- **Data Collection:** Patient surveys, genetic data, and *Electronic Health Records* (EHR) are the methods used to collect data.
- **Data Processing:** Standardizing medical language and standards is part of data processing.
- **Data Storage:** Patient data is stored in safe data warehouses.
- **Data Analysis**: Predictive analytics for evaluating the risk of disease and the effectiveness of treatment.
- **Data Visualization:** Trends in patient health are displayed on interactive dashboards for clinicians.
- **Insight Generation:** Personalized treatment regimens and early illness identification are examples of insight generation.
- **Result:** By using data to inform clinical decisions, better patient outcomes and more effective healthcare delivery are achieved.

4.3.2.3. **Financial Industry:**

- **Organization:** *JPMorgan Chase*
- **Data collection** methods include economic indicators, transaction records, and market data.
- **Data processing:** Integrating and cleansing data in real time.
- **Data Storage:** High-performance data warehouses for quick access are used for data storage.
- **Data Analysis:** Real-time analytics for risk management and fraud detection through data analysis.
- **Data visualization**: Trading and risk assessment dashboards that are updated in real time.
- **Insight Generation**: Identifying market patterns and fraud alerts is known as insight generation.
- **Result:** Through timely insights, improved risk management, decreased fraud, and improved investment strategies are achieved.

4.3.2.4. **Urban Planning:**

- **City:** *Copenhagen, Denmark*
- **Data collection** methods include environmental sensors, traffic sensors, and data from public transit.
- **Data processing** involves combining and purifying information from several city agencies.
- **Data Storage**: Urban data on a centralized platform.
- **Data Analysis:** Examining environmental and traffic data.
- **Data Visualization**: Dashboards and interactive maps for city planners.
- **Insight Generation**: Finding hotspots for traffic congestion and pollution sources is a key component of insight generation.
- **Result:** Data-driven urban planning leads to better urban mobility and lower pollution.

4.3.2.5. **Energy Industry:**

- **Business:** *GE (General Electric)*
- **Data gathering**: information from power plants, smart meters, and grid sensors.
- **Data processing:** Bringing together data from many sources.
- **Data Storage:** Cloud-based storage solutions that are scalable for data storage.
- **Data Analysis:** Predictive analytics for forecasting and maintaining energy demand.
- **Data Visualization:** Grid performance and energy consumption are tracked in real time via dashboards.
- **Insight Generation:** Knowledge of patterns in energy consumption and anticipated maintenance needs.
- **Result:** By using proactive maintenance and optimal energy distribution, energy efficiency is increased and operational expenses are decreased.

In summary, it takes a number of steps to turn data into insights, including meticulous data gathering, processing, storing, analysis, visualization, and interpretation. To make sure that the data is precise, pertinent, and usable, each stage is essential. Organizations in a variety of industries can use big data to drive strategic goals, obtain insightful information, and make well-informed decisions by following this procedure. The above examples show how several sectors successfully convert data into useful insights that can be implemented to enhance operations, boost consumer happiness, and gain a competitive edge

# Chapter 5: The Power of Artificial Intelligence and Machine Learning

## 5.1. AI in Urban Management

The principle behind the application of artificial intelligence (AI) is to maximize, simplify, and broaden the scope of even the most complex processes. Their systems are designed to recognize patterns, make decisions and predictions, and respond quickly and precisely when necessary. The amount and quality of data, which may be collected via apps, cameras, and sensors, determines how effective the models are. Artificial intelligence-based urban technology has been viewed as a means of enhancing city management, particularly in denser and larger-scale urban environments.

Smart cities are frequently linked to the idea of artificial intelligence. These cities share certain characteristics in theory and practice, even though their definitions differ, such as the application of technologies and management techniques meant to improve citizen quality of life and boost resource and service efficiency. These tactics are frequently connected with terminology like artificial intelligence, machine learning, big data, and the internet of things (IoT).

In this regard, there may be a close relationship between artificial intelligence, bettering urban systems, and municipal management. However, it's also critical to understand the actual demands of city dwellers and how AI may help to enhance urban environments. Involving the community is also essential to fostering public trust in the systems and encouraging action to address potential problems.

Urban management is changing dramatically as a result of artificial intelligence (AI), which is providing new resources and approaches to difficult urban problems. In urban management, artificial intelligence is having a major impact in the following areas:

5.1.1. **Smart Infrastructure and Maintenance:** Predictive maintenance of urban infrastructure, including utility networks, bridges, and roadways, is made possible by AI. In order to anticipate possible problems and improve maintenance schedules, *artificial intelligence (AI) algorithms analyze real-time data on structural health collected by sensors installed in infrastructure.* This minimizes disruptions, lowers expenses, and increases the longevity of infrastructure.

5.1.2. **Transportation and Traffic Management:** Through adaptive traffic signal regulation and real-time monitoring, artificial intelligence improves traffic management. *Artificial intelligence (AI) systems can increase the efficiency of public transit, optimize traffic flow, and lessen congestion by evaluating data from a variety of sources, such as cameras, sensors, and GPS devices.* AI-powered autonomous cars are also poised to transform urban mobility by providing safer and more effective modes of transit.

5.1.3. **Sustainability and Energy Management**: Artificial Intelligence facilitates the creation of smart grids that combine renewable energy sources and increase energy efficiency. *Artificial Intelligence contributes to cost savings and waste reduction by anticipating patterns in energy usage and improving distribution.* AI-powered systems are also capable of controlling city lighting more effectively, modifying brightness in response to current data in order to save energy.

5.1.4. **Security and Safety for the Public**: Predictive policing is one use of AI in public safety, where computers examine crime data to find trends and hotspots, allowing for more proactive and efficient law enforcement. *Urban security can be improved* *by AI-powered surveillance systems that can identify odd activity and instantly notify the appropriate authorities.*

5.1.5. **Development and Planning of Urban Areas:** By evaluating enormous datasets pertaining to population expansion, land usage, and environmental effects, artificial intelligence (AI) helps urban planners make data-driven decisions. *AI models can mimic the results of various planning scenarios, assisting planners in creating more resilient and sustainable urban designs.* AI is also capable of optimizing land usage by determining the ideal sites for new developments by taking into account a variety of factors.

5.1.6. **Waste Management**: By evaluating data to optimize collection routes and schedules, artificial intelligence (AI) enhances waste collection and recycling processes. *Waste management services can be informed via smart bins with sensors when they need to be emptied, which lowers overflow and increases productivity.* AI can also aid in more efficient recycling rate sorting of recyclables.

5.1.7. **Environmental Management and Monitoring:** By analyzing data from multiple sources, including sensors and satellite photos, *AI improves environmental monitoring by keeping track of noise pollution, air and water quality, and other environmental variables.* As a result, urban settings can be made healthier by addressing pollution and other environmental problems in a timely manner.

5.1.8. **Services and Citizen Engagement**: Artificial intelligence (AI)-driven chatbots and virtual assistants enhance public engagement by offering prompt information and support. *Routine queries can be handled by these systems, freeing up human resources for more difficult jobs.* AI may also evaluate input from the public to pinpoint regions that require development, facilitating inclusive and responsive urban governance.

5.1.9. **Challenges and Considerations:**

Notwithstanding its advantages, incorporating AI into urban administration comes with several drawbacks, such as:

a. **Data Security and Privacy:** Preserving the rights of citizens requires safeguarding the security and privacy of data gathered from metropolitan areas.

b. **Fairness and Bias:** AI systems need to be developed and trained to steer clear of biases that can result in the unjust treatment of particular demographic groups.

c. **Accountability and Transparency**: There should be procedures in place to hold AI systems accountable as well as transparent decision-making processes.

In summary, Artificial Intelligence (AI) is a potent instrument for urban management that provides creative ways to raise sustainability, efficiency, and standard of living in cities. Urban planners and administrators may design smarter, more resilient urban settings that satisfy the requirements of their residents by tackling the difficulties and utilizing the advantages of AI.

## 5.2. Machine Learning Applications in Smart Cities

A branch of artificial intelligence called *Machine Learning* (ML) *focuses on creating systems that can learn from data and get better over time.* Machine learning applications play a critical role in optimizing urban management, improving the standard of living, and increasing the sustainability of cities in the context of smart cities. ML is being used in smart cities in the following important areas:

5.2.1. **Predictive Infrastructure Maintenance**: Machine learning algorithms are capable of analyzing sensor data implanted in infrastructure to forecast when repair is required. For instance, *machine learning (ML) in smart grids can anticipate equipment failures and plan pro-active maintenance to avoid outages and lower repair costs.* This program improves the resilience and security of urban infrastructure, including highways, bridges, and buildings.

5.2.2. **Optimization and Traffic Management:** To optimize traffic flow, machine learning algorithms process data from sensors, GPS units, and traffic cameras. *ML can modify traffic signal timings and recommend alternate routes by forecasting traffic patterns and congestion.* As a result, travel times are shortened, emissions are decreased, and transportation networks operate more efficiently overall. Additionally, by improving their navigation and decision-making abilities, ML can aid in the development of autonomous cars.

5.2.3. **Smart Grids and Energy Consumption:** Machine learning (ML) can estimate energy supply and demand in smart grids, improving energy distribution and cutting waste. *Machine learning models aid in the integration of renewable energy sources by forecasting their output and modifying the grid in response. As a result,* *load is balanced and downtime is reduced, ensuring a steady and sustainable energy supply.*

5.2.4. **Environmental Management and Monitoring:** *Data from weather stations, water quality monitors, and air quality sensors are analyzed using machine learning algorithms.* These models have the ability to forecast pollution levels, pinpoint the sources of pollution, and recommend mitigating techniques. For example, cities can give warnings and take preventive action to safeguard public health when ML is used to forecast smog episodes.

5.2.5. **Crime Prevention and Public Safety**: By using machine learning to analyze crime data and find trends and hotspots, public safety is improved. *With the use of predictive policing models, law enforcement may more efficiently deploy resources by predicting crime hotspots.* Furthermore, real-time alerting of authorities and the detection of suspicious activity are two further benefits of ML-powered surveillance systems, which speed up response times and discourage illegal activity.

5.2.6. **Optimization of Waste Management:** By examining data on garbage output and bin fill levels, machine learning can optimize waste collection routes. This *lessens the impact on the environment, guarantees prompt collection, and uses less fuel.* By more precisely and effectively identifying recyclable materials, ML models also enhance recycling procedures and raise recycling rates.

5.2.7. **Development and Planning in Urban Areas**: Big datasets, such as those pertaining to land use, transportation, and demographic trends, are analyzed by urban planners using machine learning. By simulating the effects of different urban growth scenarios, *ML models can assist planners in making well-informed decisions.* Better resource allocation, more effective land use, and sustainable urban growth are the results of this.

5.2.8. **Smart Building Management:** Building operations, such as HVAC (*Heating, Ventilation, And Air Conditioning*) and lighting systems, are optimized by machine learning algorithms. *Machine Learning (ML) is able to make real-time adjustments to these systems to increase occupant comfort and energy efficiency by learning from occupancy patterns and ambient variables.* As a result, energy expenses are decreased and urban building sustainability is improved.

5.2.9. **Engagement and Services for Citizens:** Through the use of chatbots and virtual assistants that offer assistance and information, machine learning improves citizen services. *Over time, these systems get better at responding as a result of learning from encounters.* Furthermore, ML may examine user comments to pinpoint areas where municipal services need to be improved, promoting more responsive and participatory urban governance.

5.2.10. **Challenges and Considerations:** Despite all of its advantages, machine learning (ML) in smart cities presents several obstacles as well.

    a. **Data Availability and Quality:** Robust, high-quality data is essential to the success of machine learning models. Making sure data is accessible and accurate is important.

    b. **Data Security and Privacy** are issues that are brought up by the fact that machine learning systems frequently call for massive volumes of data. Enough safeguards must be in place to preserve the privacy of citizens.

    c. **Fairness and Bias:** ML models may carry over biases from the data, producing unjust results. It's crucial to guarantee inclusion and fairness in ML applications.

    d. **Integration and Scalability**: It takes a lot of cooperation and funding to scale machine learning solutions to citywide applications and integrate them into the current urban infrastructure.

In summary, the foundation of smart city efforts is machine learning, which offers cutting-edge instruments to maximize sustainability, optimize urban administration, and raise living standards. Cities may fully utilize machine learning (ML) to build more resilient, efficient, and livable urban environments by tackling the related obstacles.

## 5.3.  Predictive Analytics and Urban Planning

Utilizing data analysis, statistical algorithms, and machine learning approaches, *predictive analytics is a potent instrument in urban planning that projects future patterns and events.* Experts in both IT and urban planning, can tell you how predictive analytics is changing the field of urban planning:

5.3.1. **Development and Maintenance of Infrastructure**: Infrastructure requirements can be predicted using predictive analytics using data on population increase, urbanization patterns, and economic growth. *Urban planners can forecast the locations of new highways, bridges, schools, and hospitals by examining past data and contemporary patterns.* In order to prevent infrastructure breakdowns, predictive models can also forecast maintenance requirements and help prioritize repairs and improvements.

5.3.2. **Planning for Transportation:** By predicting traffic patterns, public transportation utilization, and the effects of new transportation projects, predictive analytics aids in the optimization of transportation networks. *Predictive models can locate hotspots for traffic congestion, peak travel periods, and possible future demand by evaluating data from traffic sensors, GPS devices, and public transportation systems.* This makes it possible for planners to create transportation networks that are more accessible and have shorter trip times.

5.3.3. **Real Estate and Housing Development:** Predictive analytics is a tool used by urban planners to predict housing demand and real estate market trends. *Predictive models can pinpoint locations with potential for residential development by examining demographic data, economic indicators, and housing market trends.* This aids in the design of new housing developments, guarantees a sufficient supply, and avoids overbuilding or housing shortages.

5.3.4. **Sustainability and Environmental Planning**: Environmental planning relies heavily on predictive analytics to assist cities manage resources and lessen the environmental effects of urbanization. *Climate change effects, the quality of the air and water, and the consequences of new advances on natural resources can all be predicted using predictive models.* This enables planners to create strategies for climate resilience, build green infrastructure, and implement sustainable behaviors.

5.3.5. **Development of the Economy**: The application of predictive analytics to identify growth prospects and potential obstacles promotes economic development. *Predictive models are used to identify industries with growth potential and forecast economic conditions by studying business activity, employment trends, and economic statistics.* This supports planners in luring capital, generating employment, and formulating plans for long-term, steady economic expansion.

5.3.6. **Safety and Public Health**: By predicting disease outbreaks, the need for emergency response, and patterns of criminal activity, predictive analytics improves public health and safety. *Predictive models can pinpoint regions by examining health statistics, socioeconomic variables, and environmental factors.* Similar to this, crime data analysis may be used to identify crime hotspots, which helps law enforcement better allocate resources and proactively address public safety issues.

5.3.7. **Budgeting and Resource Allocation**: Urban planners can more effectively manage budgets and allocate resources when they use predictive analytics. *Predictive models provide for more precise resource allocation and budgeting by* *projecting future demands for services like waste management, electricity, and water supply.* This guarantees that cities won't have to use more resources than necessary to meet demands in the future.

5.3.8. **Community Involvement and Engagement**: Using predictive analytics to spot patterns in public opinion and involvement, community engagement can be improved. *Predictive models can determine the preferences and concerns of the community by examining social media, surveys, and comments from open consultations.* This enables planners to anticipate problems and create initiatives that complement the goals and objectives of the community.

5.3.9. **Challenges and Considerations:** Predictive analytics has many advantages, but it also has drawbacks.

   a. **Data Availability and Quality:** Comprehensive, high-quality data are necessary for precise forecasts. It is vital to guarantee the availability and integrity of data.

   b. **Data Security and Privacy** are issues that are brought up by the use of big datasets. Sensitive data must be protected with strong protections in place.

   c. **Fairness and Bias:** Unfair results may result from predictive algorithms that absorb biases found in the data. It is crucial to guarantee inclusivity and fairness in predictive analytics.

   d. **Integration and Execution:** Considerable funding and cooperation are needed to incorporate predictive analytics into the current urban planning procedures and frameworks.

In summary, *urban planning is changing as a result of predictive analytics, which offers data-driven insights that improve strategic planning and decision-making.* Urban planners may build more resilient, effective, and sustainable cities by tackling the issues and utilizing predictive analytics

# Chapter 6: Internet of Things (IoT) in Smart Cities

## 6.1. The Need for High-Speed Connectivity in Urban Planning

The foundation of sustainable urban planning is being formed by smart cities and smart city ideas, which provide good living standards for their citizens. This emergence is mostly due to smart mobility, which enhances lifestyles and provides sustainable transportation. However, quick, secure, and dependable connectivity techniques are essential to its success.

> *The goals of IoT deployments in smart cities are to increase sustainability, facilitate the development of smart intercity transportation networks, maximize water management initiatives, and enhance the energy efficiency of public buildings and lighting. By improving a range of urban activities, including traffic flow, infrastructure maintenance, energy management, pollution control, and public safety, smart cities use the Internet of Things to improve the quality of life for their citizens – **Patrick Mukosha***

After extensive testing and trials in Europe in the late 1980s and early 1990s, smart cities are starting to spread widely. A more unified smart infrastructure has begun to emerge from early efforts that concentrated on information and communications projects, sustainable places, grid energy solutions, and data collecting utilizing *Geographic Information Systems* (GIS). Fast internet access is a must for contemporary urban planning since it is vital to the growth and operation of smart cities.

For the following main reasons, having high-speed connectivity is essential:

6.1.1. **Encouraging IoT Integration and Smart Infrastructure**: Integrating the Internet of Things (IoT) into urban infrastructure requires high-speed connectivity. For the purpose of gathering and transmitting data in real-time, *Internet of Things devices—like smart sensors, cameras, and meters—need strong and dependable internet connections*. For the purpose of managing different urban systems, such as public safety, utilities, and traffic, this data is crucial. Smart traffic signals, for example, can enhance traffic flow and lessen congestion by adjusting to real-time traffic conditions; however, their effectiveness depends on reliable and fast internet connections.

6.1.2. **Improving Citizen Engagement and Public Services**: The provision of effective governmental services and increased citizen engagement are made possible by high-speed internet. *High-speed connectivity is necessary for online platforms that provide services like e-governance, health, education, and public safety to work well.* Digital platforms allow citizens to report problems, access services, and take part in urban planning processes, increasing the responsiveness and inclusivity of governance. Telemedicine, which enables citizens to obtain medical consultations and services remotely, is also supported by high-speed internet.

6.1.3. **Encouragement of Innovation and Economic Development**: *Rapid internet access promotes innovation and economic expansion.* Because it offers the infrastructure required for big data analytics, cloud services, and high-performance computing, it draws in organizations, especially those in tech-driven industries. Reliable internet is essential for startups and digital enterprises to create and implement creative solutions. Furthermore, high-speed internet is essential for productive and seamless remote work, which is becoming more and more common.

6.1.4. **Making Data-Driven Urban Design Possible**: To make well-informed judgments about the growth and management of cities, urban planners rely on data. Large datasets may be collected, sent, and analyzed in real time with the help of high-speed internet. This makes it possible for planners to create more effective and sustainable city designs through simulations, real-time monitoring, and predictive analytics. *Real-time traffic pattern analysis, for instance, can help with the planning of new transit facilities and the improvement of current lines.*

6.1.5. **Enhancing Quality of Life:** Residents' quality of life is enhanced by high-speed internet connectivity since it gives them access to communication tools, entertainment, and information. Through the facilitation of digital classrooms and e-learning platforms, it promotes educational activities. High-speed internet promotes lifelong learning and personal growth for families and people by enabling the streaming of educational content, online courses, and access to worldwide information resources.

6.1.6. **Progressing with Environmental Sustainability**: Via more effective resource management, *high-speed connectivity can support environmental sustainability*. For example, real-time data is used by smart grids to optimize energy distribution, cut waste, and maximize the usage of renewable energy sources. In a similar vein, intelligent water management systems can save water by tracking usage and identifying leaks. The smooth functioning of these systems is made possible by high-speed internet, which helps create a more sustainable urban environment.

6.1.7. **Improving Public Safety and Emergency Response:** For public safety and emergency response systems, high-speed communication is essential. *Response times and coordination among emergency services, including police, fire, and ambulance departments, can be greatly enhanced with real-time communication and data exchange.* In order to improve public safety overall, high-speed internet is necessary for sophisticated surveillance systems, early warning systems for natural disasters, and real-time resident alerts.

6.1.8. **Challenges and Considerations:** Despite the obvious necessity for high-speed internet, there are a few issues that need to be resolved:

    a. **Infrastructure Investment:** It can be expensive to build the infrastructure required for high-speed internet, especially in underserved or densely populated urban areas.

    b. **Digital Divide:** Preventing a digital gap requires making sure that everyone in the community, even those in rural or low-income areas, has fair access to high-speed internet.

    c. **Privacy and Security:** Concerns regarding data security and privacy are raised by the volume of data transfer that high-speed internet generates. Strong cybersecurity defenses are necessary to safeguard private data.

d. **Frameworks for Regulations and Policies:** Infrastructure for high-speed internet deployment and administration requires efficient legislative and policy frameworks.

In summary, for smart cities to be developed and urban settings to be managed effectively, high-speed connectivity is essential. It promotes economic progress, advances the integration of cutting-edge technologies, improves public services, and raises citizens' standards of living. Through the resolution of issues and the utilization of high-speed internet, urban planners can establish more interconnected, effective, and sustainable urban environments.

## 6.2. 5G: The Game Changer in Urban Planning

With the ability to collect and evaluate data in real time, urban planners may now quickly adapt city services to changing needs. For instance, 5G can monitor traffic flow and congestion, allowing real-time adjustments to traffic signals and public transportation timetables. Additionally, *5G may be used to track noise levels and air quality, which will aid planners in identifying and resolving environmental issues.* With the help of 5G, sensors on traffic signals, lamps, and other infrastructure can provide data that will be utilized to enhance city services and make cities more habitable.

> *5G is transforming conventional approaches of urban planning. High-speed, low-latency connectivity is enabling real-time data analytics, interactive simulations, and agile decision-making to supplant the antiquated method of city planning, which involved static models and sporadic updates. This change is mostly caused by 5G's extraordinary speed at which it can process large volumes of data. Not only does this speed up smartphone downloads, but it also establishes a network connecting residents, automobiles, appliances, infrastructure, and city services – enabling smart cities.* **- Patrick Mukosha**

5G can help planners make better judgments about the layout and operation of cities by giving them access to real-time data. Cities that are more sustainable, livable, and efficient may result from this. 5G technology's previously unheard-of speed, connectivity, and capacity are poised to completely transform urban design.

Here are some ways that 5G will revolutionize smart cities:

6.2.1. **Low Latency and Unprecedented Speed**: When it comes to latency and speed, *5G networks are far faster than those of earlier mobile network generations*. This makes real-time data processing and communication possible, which is essential for applications like intelligent traffic control systems and autonomous cars that need to receive feedback instantly. Urban systems can communicate almost instantly thanks to 5G's low latency, which can be as low as 1 millisecond. This increases their responsiveness and efficiency.

6.2.2. **Encouraging Widespread IoT Implementation:** Significantly *more connected devices can be supported per square kilometer by 5G than by 4G networks*. This is necessary for the broad use of IoT devices in smart cities, such as energy consumption, trash management, traffic monitoring, and air quality sensors. These devices can function concurrently without network congestion because to 5G's increased bandwidth, which makes extensive data collecting and analysis possible.

6.2.3. **Strengthened Emergency Services and Public Safety**: Through enhanced data exchange and communication, *5G technology improves emergency services and public safety*. Real-time video streaming from drones, first responders' body cameras, and surveillance cameras is made possible by dependable, fast connectivity. During emergencies, this real-time information can enhance situational awareness and coordination, resulting in quicker and more efficient responses. Furthermore, 5G enables cutting-edge applications like robotics and remote-controlled emergency vehicles.

6.2.4. **Mobility and Smart Transportation**: *The growth of driverless cars and intelligent transportation systems depends on 5G*. It offers the dependable, low-latency connection required for vehicle-to-everything (V2X) connectivity, which connects automobiles to infrastructure, traffic lights, and other cars. This can facilitate effective route planning, lessen traffic accidents, and enhance traffic flow. Real-time tracking and management can also help public transportation systems by increasing service quality and punctuality.

6.2.5. **Resource Management and Energy**: *5G makes real-time utility monitoring and control possible, which makes sophisticated energy and resource management systems easier to implement*. By incorporating renewable energy sources and cutting waste, smart grids can more effectively manage the supply and demand for electricity. Water management systems are capable of identifying leaks, tracking usage trends, and optimizing distribution. These qualities support resilience and sustainability in urban infrastructure.

6.2.6. **Enhanced Life Quality Through Smart Services**: The quality of life for people is enhanced by 5G's improved delivery of smart services. *With 5G's fast and dependable connectivity, smart healthcare applications like telemedicine, remote surgery, and real-time health monitoring become more practical.* The high bandwidth of 5G can facilitate immersive learning experiences through virtual and augmented reality (VR/AR), which can be advantageous for educational services. Smart home applications and gadgets can also work together more smoothly and efficiently.

6.2.7. **Innovation and Economic Growth**: The introduction of 5G networks encourages innovation and draws in enterprises, which both boost economic growth. *Entrepreneurs, tech firms, and sectors dependent on cutting-edge technologies are more inclined to make investments in regions with strong 5G infrastructure.* This encourages the creation of new goods and services and opens up job opportunities. In addition, 5G makes it feasible for previously unfeasible new applications and business models including smart manufacturing, industrial automation, and sophisticated robots.

6.2.8. **Better Urban Development and Planning**: 5G gives planners access to real-time data and sophisticated analytical tools, which facilitates more efficient urban planning and development. *5G-enabled sensors and devices can be used by planners to model different growth scenarios, keep an eye on urban conditions, and make data-driven decisions.* Real-time information on air quality, energy consumption, and traffic patterns, for instance, can help designers create more sustainable and effective urban environments. Applications for augmented reality (AR) can also assist in seeing and simulating the effects of new initiatives prior to deployment.

6.2.9. **Challenges and Considerations:** Although 5G has many advantages, there are a few issues that must be resolved before it can be successfully implemented in urban planning:

  a. **Infrastructure Investment:** Installing fiber optic cables, tiny cells, and improved base stations are just a few of the infrastructure-related costs associated with the rollout of 5G networks.

  b. **Frameworks for Regulations and Policies**: For 5G to be widely adopted, efficient legislative and policy frameworks—including those pertaining to spectrum allocation and site approvals—are required.

c.  **Data Security and Privacy**: Data security and privacy are becoming more and more important as linked devices and data transfer grow. Strong cybersecurity defenses are necessary to safeguard private data.

d.  **Digital Divide:** Preventing a digital divide between various socioeconomic classes and geographic areas requires ensuring equitable access to 5G technologies.

In summary, 5G is a game-changing technology that might completely change smart city development and urban planning. 5G provides sophisticated applications and services that improve the efficiency, sustainability, and livability of urban areas by offering high-speed, low-latency, and high-capacity connection. To fully enjoy the advantages of 5G and build more inventive, resilient, and connected cities, it will be imperative to address the related issues.

## 6.3.  Future Connectivity Solutions

Advanced connectivity solutions are becoming more and more necessary as cities transform into smart urban environments. As urban systems become more sophisticated, future connectivity solutions will expand on current technology, such as 5G, by adding new capabilities and paradigms. The following significant future connection innovations will influence urban planning:

6.3.1.  **Networks with 6G**: The next generation of wireless technology, or 6G, is expected to replace 5G. *6G is anticipated to launch in the 2030s and will provide even faster internet speeds, less latency, and wider coverage.* With latency of less than 1 millisecond and possible rates of up to 1 terabit per second (Tbps), 6G will make it possible to use cutting-edge applications like holographic communications, immersive *Extended Reality* (XR), and pervasive AI.

- **Important Characteristics:**
    a.  **Terabit Data Rates**: These allow real-time data analytics, sophisticated VR/AR applications, and streaming of extremely high resolution video.
    b.  **Sub-Millisecond Latency**: Enabling real-time uses including industrial automation, driverless vehicles, and remote surgery.
    c.  **Enhanced Connectivity Density**: Enabling trillions of sensors, IoT devices, and smart infrastructure elements to be integrated.

6.3.2. **Internet Via Satellite:** Terrestrial networks will be complemented by satellite internet technologies, particularly with developments like Low Earth Orbit (LEO) satellite constellations. Global high-speed internet coverage is a goal of businesses like SpaceX's Starlink and Amazon's Project Kuiper, which both intend to serve remote and urban locations where traditional infrastructure is difficult to implement.

- **Important Characteristics**:
    a. **Global Coverage:** Providing redundancy for terrestrial networks and ensuring connectivity in underdeveloped metropolitan regions.
    b. **High-Speed Access:** Providing competitive speeds appropriate for the majority of urban applications, including as gaming, streaming, and instant messaging.
    c. **Resilience:** Having a dependable backup plan in place in case of infrastructural failures or natural disasters is resilience.

6.3.3. **Network Meshes:** Mesh networks are made up of linked nodes that speak with one another directly, forming a decentralized network. They are especially helpful in urban settings for improving connectivity in homes, public areas, and during events.

- **Important Characteristics**:
    a. **Self-Healing:** Nodes make sure the network is always available by automatically rerouting traffic in the event of a connection failure.
    b. **Scalability:** The ability to add nodes quickly and easily without requiring major infrastructure upgrades.
    c. **Cost-Effectiveness:** Less need for centralized infrastructure and substantial cabling.

6.3.4. **Edge Computing:** Rather of depending on centralized cloud servers, edge computing moves data processing closer to the source of data generation (e.g., sensors, devices). This lowers bandwidth consumption and latency, which is important for real-time applications in smart cities.

- **Important Characteristics**:
    a. **Reduced Latency:** Essential for real-time applications like industrial automation, smart traffic signals, and driverless cars.
    b. **Bandwidth Optimisation:** Reduces the quantity of data transferred to centralized servers through bandwidth optimization, which lowers expenses and boosts productivity.

c. **Enhanced Security**: Local processing reduces the dangers involved in sending data across large distances.

6.3.5. **Networks of Quantum Communication**: Quantum entanglement is used in quantum communication to send data instantly and securely over great distances. Although this technology is still in the experimental phase, it offers unmatched speed and security.

- **Important Characteristics**:
    a. **Unbreakable Security:** Sensitive urban data is protected robustly by quantum encryption, which is supposedly unbreakable.
    b. **Instantaneous Transmission**: The ability to communicate instantly over long distances could improve real-time applications.

6.3.6. **Expansion of Fiber Optics:** Fiber optics continue to be the foundation of high-speed connectivity despite the importance of wireless technologies because of its great capacity and dependability. The increasing data needs of smart cities will be supported by expanding fiber optic networks.

- **Important Characteristics:**
    a. **High Bandwidth:** Able to manage enormous volumes of data; necessary for cloud services, data centers, and high-speed internet.
    b. **Low latency and High Reliability:** Perfect for vital metropolitan applications including emergency services, healthcare, and finance transactions due to its low latency and high reliability.
    c. **Future-Proofing**: Fiber infrastructure is capable of handling updates and changing technological requirements in the future.

6.3.7. **Hybrid Networks Solutions**: Several connectivity technologies combined can offer a network with strong, dependable, and extensive coverage. To provide seamless connectivity, hybrid solutions can take advantage of the advantages of many technologies (such as fiber optics, 5G, and Wi-Fi 6).

- **Important Characteristics:**
    a. **Redundancy:** Several network architectures offer redundancy in the event that one fails, guaranteeing uninterrupted connectivity.
    b. **Enhanced Efficiency and Performance:** Various technologies can be applied to certain applications to enhance efficiency and performance.
    c. **Scalability and Flexibility:** Capable of effortlessly adjusting to evolving urban requirements and technological breakthroughs.

6.3.8. **Challenges and Considerations:** There are various difficulties in putting these future networking possibilities into practice:

1. **Investment and Cost:** The development of infrastructure and the implementation of new technologies necessitate large financial investments.
2. **Regulatory and Policy Concerns**: For implementation to proceed smoothly, it is essential to guarantee adherence to regulations and create policies that support them.
3. **Privacy and Security:** To safeguard data and privacy, advanced connectivity solutions need to include strong cybersecurity safeguards.
4. **Digital Divide:** To prevent the digital divide from getting worse, equitable access to cutting-edge connectivity technologies must be guaranteed.

In summary, urban planning is about to undergo a radical change because to future connection technologies including 6G, increased fiber optics, edge computing, quantum communication, mesh networks, and satellite internet. These technological advancements will lay the groundwork for smart cities that are more habitable, efficient, and resilient. Urban planners and legislators can take use of these developments to build inclusive, sustainable, and networked urban environments by tackling the related issues

# Chapter 7: Sustainable Energy Solutions for Smart Cities

## 7.1. Integrating Renewable Energy

It has long been known that sophisticated methods are required to manage and coordinate the wide range of supply and conversion technologies as well as demand applications within the framework of the Smart City. Embedded computational intelligence algorithms and the widespread proliferation of sensors can assist in addressing many of the technological obstacles related to this energy systems integration issue.

However, obstacles persist because appropriate techniques are required to manage intricate networks of players, frequently with conflicting goals, and to make judgments about the design and operation of systems spanning a broad range of characteristics and time horizons.

The process of integrating renewable energy into the current energy infrastructure is complex and includes aspects related to technology, economy, society, and regulations. The following is a thorough summary of the essential elements and approaches for incorporating renewable energy sources—such as solar, wind, hydro, and biomass—into the electrical grid:

### 7.1.1. **Integration of Regulation and Policy:**
#### 7.1.1.1. **Regulatory Structures:**

- **Renewable Portfolio Standards (RPS):** Utility companies are required by the RPS to get a specific proportion of their energy from renewable sources.
- **Licensing and Permitting**: Streamlining the application and licensing procedures for renewable energy projects is the goal of licensing and permitting.

### 7.1.1.2. Long-Term Planning:

- **Integrated Resource Planning (IRP):** Utility and regulatory agencies' long-term planning that includes targets for renewable energy.

## 7.1.2. Economic Integration

### 7.1.2.1. Grants & Incentive Programs:

- **Feed-in Tariffs (FiTs):** Guaranteed rates of payment to producers of renewable energy to encourage investment.
- **Tax Credits:** Granting tax credits for the installation and generation of renewable energy.

### 7.1.2.2. Market Design:

- **Energy Markets:** Creating energy markets that place a premium on the adaptability and supplementary services that renewable energy sources offer.
- **Carbon Pricing:** By putting carbon pricing mechanisms into place, fossil fuels' environmental costs will be internalized, making renewable energy more affordable.

## 7.1.3. Technical Integration:

### 7.1.3.1. Grid Modernization:

- **Smart Grids:** Putting smart grids into practice to integrate variable renewable energy sources (VREs), improve dependability, and improve grid management.
- **Energy storage:** Using battery storage devices to store extra energy, maintain power in case of emergency, and balance supply and demand.
- **Grid Flexibility**: Using technologies like demand response and sophisticated forecasting, the grid may be made more flexible to meet the variable nature of renewable energy.

## 7.1.4. Distributed Generation:

- **Micro-Grids:** To improve resilience and reliability, develop micro-grids that can function either independently or in tandem with the main grid.
- **Rooftop Solar:** Promoting the installation of rooftop solar panels as a means of reducing transmission losses and decentralizing energy generation.

### 7.1.5. Standards for Interconnection:

- **Harmonizing Standards**: To guarantee dependability and safety, technical standards must be established and standardized before connecting renewable energy installations to the grid.

### 7.1.6. Integration of the Social and Environmental Domains:

#### 7.1.6.1. Public Involvement:

- **Education & Outreach:** Bringing communities into the planning process and educating them about the advantages of renewable energy.
- **Community Ownership:** To boost public support and investment, community-owned renewable energy projects should be encouraged.

#### 7.1.6.2. Environmental Factors to Be Considered:

- **Sustainable Siting:** Assuring the placement of renewable energy installations to reduce their negative effects on the environment and protect delicate ecosystems.

### 7.1.7. Problems and Solutions:

#### 7.1.7.1. Intermittency and Variability:

- **Remedy:** The use of energy storage devices, sophisticated forecasting methods, and grid flexibility strategies to balance supply and demand are the solutions.

#### 7.1.7.2. Infrastructure Upgrades:

- **Remedy:** The answer is to spend money upgrading the grid's substations and transmission lines to handle more renewable energy capacity.

#### 7.1.7.3. Market Restrictions:

- **Remedy:** Restructuring market systems to give renewable energy a fair chance at competition and doing away with fossil fuel subsidies are the two ways to solve this problem.

In summary, a comprehensive strategy that tackles the technological, financial, sociological, and regulatory obstacles involved is needed to integrate renewable energy into the current energy system. It is feasible to make the shift to a more resilient and sustainable energy future by utilizing cutting-edge technologies, establishing enabling regulations, and involving stakeholders.

## 7.2. Smart Grids and Energy Management

In order to handle the growing integration of renewable energy sources and increase overall energy efficiency, upgrading the power grid through the use of smart grids and energy management systems is essential. This is a thorough rundown of energy management and smart grids.

### 7.2.1. The Importance of Energy Management:

In a world where energy consumption is rising, power generation ought to develop in tandem to meet user demands and enhance everyday living. However, power demand may present difficulties for the electric utilities and system operators due to the growing number of consumers as well as the unpredictable nature of the electric load. Excessive peak demands are likely to happen frequently and could jeopardize the system's ability to function. The electric utility and system operators have two options to address this problem:

- Use energy management to lessen the likelihood of high peak demand during peak hours.
- Expand the network's size and scope, which will cost money and take time to deploy.

Although the first option seems more sensible, it can't manage energy without complex algorithms and techniques. For a smarter grid, energy management is deemed essential for several reasons:

- It provides precise outcomes and forecasts.
- It safeguards the climate and lowers pollutants.
- It improves energy effectiveness.
- It preserves the materials.
- It assists the system operator in cutting down on energy losses on the lines and network, which might significantly lower the cost of indirect distribution electricity.
- Since it's automated, people don't need to become involved directly.
- It assists the electric utility in lowering the cost of generation and better optimizing the performance of its generating units.
- By raising the load factor, the power profile becomes less erratic and more smooth.
- It aids consumers in controlling their load demand and lowering their electricity costs.

**7.2.2. Smart Grids:**

**7.2.2.1.  Definition and Features:** Modern technologies are integrated into smart grids to improve the sustainability, efficiency, and dependability of electrical services. Important characteristics consist of:

**7.2.2.2.  Advanced Metering Infrastructure (AMI):** With the help of real-time energy usage data from smart meters, billing accuracy and demand response can be improved.

**7.2.2.3.  Bidirectional Communication:** Smart grids, as opposed to traditional grids, provide two-way communication between utilities and customers, enabling real-time control and monitoring.

**7.2.2.4.  Control and Automation:** Systems with automated fault separation, restoration, and self-healing capabilities increase dependability and decrease downtime.

**7.2.2.5.  Integration of Renewable Energy:** Smart grids smoothly combine different renewable energy sources, using cutting-edge forecasting and real-time data to balance supply and demand.

**7.2.3. Advantages:**

**7.2.3.1.  Increased Adaptability and Resilience:** Power outages occur less frequently and last longer when there is effective load balancing and faster reaction to outages.

**7.2.3.2.** **Energy Effectiveness**: Reductions in system losses and more effective energy distribution are the results of improved monitoring and control.

**7.2.3.3.** **Customer Involvement:** Thanks to mobile apps and online portals, consumers have more visibility and control over how much energy they use, which enables them to make more informed energy decisions.

**7.2.3.4.** **Advantages for the Environment:** Through the increased adoption of renewable energy sources, smart grids contribute to a decrease in greenhouse gas emissions and a decreased dependency on fossil fuels.

### 7.2.4. Energy Management Systems (EMS):

Electric appliances and generators were traditionally operated manually or with the aid of simple control systems. These days, it's easier to control the load thanks to the development of computer-based control systems, highly efficient smart algorithms, and the integration of information and communication technologies into the power grid.

**7.2.4.1.** **Definition of and Their Components:** Systems for managing energy use, distribution, and production are optimized. EMS components consist of:

**7.2.4.2.** **Energy Tracking:** Measuring energy consumption and performance indicators continuously across various processes and systems.

**7.2.4.3.** **Analysis of Energy:** Sophisticated analytics to find trends, inefficiencies, and areas where energy can be saved.

**7.2.4.4.** **Control Systems:** Automated controls to optimize energy use based on pre-established settings and real-time data for HVAC, lighting, and other systems.

**7.2.4.5.** **Reaction to Demand:** initiatives aimed at encouraging consumers to shift or cut back on their energy use at times of peak demand in order to save costs and improve grid stability.

### 7.2.5. Advantages

**7.2.5.1.** **Savings on costs:** Optimizing energy use can result in significant savings on energy bills and lower operating costs.

**7.2.5.2.** **Sustainability:** Enhancing energy efficiency and using renewable energy sources help achieve sustainability objectives while lessening their negative effects on the environment.

**7.2.5.3.** **Efficiency of Operations**: Operations and maintenance become more efficient with improved management and monitoring.

**7.2.5.4. Compliance:** By assisting companies in adhering to energy legislation and standards, EMS may help them avoid fines and penalties.

### 7.2.6. Energy Management Systems:

The following list includes some of the most popular control systems:

- Automation Systems (such as those for homes, offices, etc.)
- Energy Management System (EMS);
- Building Management System (BMS);
- Programmable Logic Controller (PLC);
- Supervisory Control and Data Acquisition (SCADA);

These are computer-based control systems, and for them to function, hardware and software are needed. Typically, engineers, software developers, or specialists write the software code. Typically, the hardware has inputs and outputs that allow the system to control the power consumption or turn on and off some of the associated parts.

### 7.2.7. Integrating EMS and Smart Grids:

The performance of the energy infrastructure as a whole is improved when smart grids and energy management systems are integrated. This integration consists of:

**7.2.7.1. Analytics and Data Sharing:** Smart grid real-time data can be incorporated into EMS to improve forecasting and energy management.

**7.2.7.2. Coordinated Control:** Network-wide energy consumption can be maximized by coordinated control mechanisms between the grid and end users.

**7.2.7.3. Improved Reaction to Demand:** Grid stability can be increased and peak loads can be decreased with improved demand response algorithms that make use of automated controls and real-time data.

**7.2.7.4. Preventive Maintenance:** Predictive analytics may anticipate possible problems and enable proactive maintenance, which lowers downtime and increases equipment lifespan.

### 7.2.8. Problems and Solutions:

### 7.2.8.1. Cybersecurity:

- **Solution:** The answer is to put strong cybersecurity measures in place, such as intrusion detection systems, encryption, and frequent security audits.

### 7.2.8.2. Data Privacy:

- **Solution:** To protect customer information and adhere to regulations, make sure that stringent data privacy measures are in place.

**7.2.8.3. Interoperability:**

- **Solution:** The answer is to create and implement standards to guarantee system and technology interoperability.

**7.2.8.4. Exorbitant Starting Costs:**

- **Solution:** The answer is to control costs and show value through phased adoption, public-private partnerships, and government incentives.

In summary, energy management programs and smart grids will be essential elements of the energy landscape of the future. They enable consumers to more efficiently monitor their energy usage and facilitate the incorporation of renewable energy sources by enhancing efficiency, reliability, and sustainability. To reach their full potential, addressing the issues through cooperation, policy, and technology will be essential.

## 7.3. Promoting Energy Efficiency

One of the most important tactics for cutting greenhouse gas emissions, energy consumption, and reaching sustainability targets is to promote energy efficiency. Clearly, some nations are making good strides toward accelerating energy efficiency. The best achievement appears to come from creative financing partnerships with central banks, multilateral banks, and financial markets, as well as supportive governance and regulatory environments that promote local financial institutions. The array of tangible policies and initiatives that encourage and enable customers, local governments, utilities, and service providers to promote energy efficiency results can be broadened and deepened.

Improvements in service quantity and quality as well as a decrease in energy consumption are the two main results of energy efficiency investments. The truth is that significant gains in productivity and welfare have frequently gone unrecognized because energy efficiency is foolishly mistaken for "saving energy." As a result, service enhancements are frequently disregarded.

Here's a detailed examination of the numerous strategies used to advance energy efficiency in various industries:

**7.3.1. Residential Sector**

**7.3.1.1. Strategies**

1.  **Energy-Efficient Appliances:**
    - **Labeling Initiatives:** Putting in place and advocating for labeling initiatives such as Energy Star, which designate and promote the usage of energy-efficient equipment.
    - **Rewards:** offering tax breaks, rebates, and other incentives to consumers who buy energy-efficient equipment and appliances.
2.  **Standards and Codes for Construction:**
    - **Updated Codes:** Implementing strict energy standards and building rules that mandate significant repairs and new construction to meet high energy efficiency requirements.
    - **Retrofitting:** Providing financial incentives and assistance to renovate old buildings in order to upgrade their HVAC, windows, and insulation.
3.  **Technology for Smart Homes:**
    - **Home Automation:** Promoting the use of intelligent lights, appliances, thermostats, and other devices that can be managed and enhanced by home automation systems.
    - **Energy monitoring:** supplying instruments and applications that enable households to track and control their energy consumption in real time.
    - **Advantages**
        a. **Cost savings:** Lower energy costs for residential users.
        b. **Comfort and Health**: Better air quality and interior comfort.
        c. **Environmental Impact:** Less stress on the electrical grid and a decrease in greenhouse gas emissions.

### 7.3.2. Commercial Industry

### 7.3.2.1. Strategies

1.  **Audits of Energy:**
    - **Frequent Audits:** To find inefficiencies and chances for improvement in commercial buildings, conduct routine energy audits.
    - **Action Plans:** Creating and carrying out plans of action in response to audit results.
2.  **Energy-Efficient Lighting and HVAC systems:**

- **LED Lighting:** Energy-efficient LED lighting can take the place of conventional lighting.
- **HVAC Upgrades**: For improved performance, switching to high-efficiency HVAC systems and incorporating cutting-edge controls.

3. **Building Management Systems (BMS):**
   - **Automation:** Using BMS to optimize and automate building systems such as lighting, HVAC, and air conditioning.
   - **Real-time monitoring**: Using data in real-time to make well-informed decisions regarding maintenance and energy use.
   - **Advantages**
     a. **Operational Savings:** Reduced spending for operations and energy.
     b. **Enhanced Work circumstances:** Enhanced working circumstances result in higher worker productivity.
     c. **Sustainability Objectives:** Improved standing and adherence to rules and guidelines.

## 7.3.3. Industrial Sector

## 7.3.3.1. Strategies:

1. **Process Optimisation:**
   - **Efficient Processes:** Energy-efficient technologies and methods should be used in manufacturing and production.
   - **Continuous Improvement**: Increasing energy efficiency over time by implementing techniques like Six Sigma and Lean.

2. **Energy Management Systems:**
   - **ISO 50001:** To systematically increase energy performance, energy management standards such as ISO 50001 should be adopted.
   - **Real-time Data:** Optimizing energy utilization in industrial operations with real-time data and analytics.

3. **Recovering Waste Heat:**

- **Heat Exchangers:** Installing heat exchangers and other technologies to collect and recycle waste heat from industrial processes is known as heat exchanger installation.
- **Advantages**
    a. **Cost Reduction**: Significant energy cost savings as well as increased competitiveness.
    b. **Environmental Compliance:** Reducing carbon footprint and adhering to environmental rules.
    c. **Resource Efficiency:** Waste reduction and more effective use of resources.

## 7.3.4. Transportation Sector:

## 7.3.4.1.  Strategies:

1. **Standards for Fuel Efficiency:**
    - **Vehicle Standards:** Establishing and upholding requirements for automobiles' fuel economy
    - **Programs for eco-driving:** Encouraging fuel-efficient driving practices.

2. **Public Transport:**
    - **Investment:** Making large-scale, effective investments in public transportation networks.
    - **Incentives:** Offering discounts on tickets and employer-sponsored transit passes as inducements to use public transportation.

3. **Electric Vehicles (EVs):**
    - **Incentives:** Offering financial incentives to encourage the use and purchase of hybrid and electric cars.
    - **Infrastructure for Charging**: Increasing infrastructure for charging EVs in order to facilitate their wider adoption.
    - **Advantages**
        a. **Lower Fuel Costs:** Both households and companies will pay less for fuel.
        b. **Improvements in Air Quality:** Lower levels of air pollution and related health advantages.

c. **Energy Independence:** Reduced dependency on fossil fuels and improved energy security are two aspects of energy independence.

## 7.3.5. Policy and Regulatory Approaches

### 7.3.5.1. Strategies

1. **Energy Efficiency Guidelines:**
   - **Regulations:** Creating and revising energy-efficiency requirements for buildings, cars, and appliances.
   - **Compliance:** Ensuring compliance by means of periodic inspections and enforcement protocols.

2. **Monetary Rewards:**
   - **Grants and Loans**: Offering low-interest loans, grants, and other forms of financial support to energy-saving initiatives.
   - **Tax Credits:** Providing tax breaks for projects and improvements that use less energy.

3. **Campaigns for Public Awareness:**
   - **Education Programs:** Holding public awareness events to inform businesses and customers about the advantages of energy conservation.
   - **Partnerships:** collaborating on energy-saving projects with stakeholders, NGOs, and business associations.
   - **Advantages**
     a. **Market transformation** is the process of establishing incentives and priorities for energy efficiency.
     b. **Innovation:** Promoting creativity and the creation of novel, energy-saving methods and technology.
     c. **Economic Growth**: Promoting economic growth by reducing energy use and creating jobs in the energy-efficient industry.

In summary, technology developments, laws, financial incentives, and public involvement all play a part in promoting energy efficiency. Through the implementation of these solutions, several industries can attain noteworthy reductions in energy consumption, expenses, and ecological advantages, thereby augmenting the prospects of a sustainable and robust energy landscape.

# Chapter 8: Revolutionising Transportation Systems

## 8.1. Smart Public Transit Systems: A Bridging of Technology and Urban Design

Information technology and urban planning are combined in smart public transit systems to improve the effectiveness, accessibility, and sustainability of public transportation networks. These systems take advantage of developments in real-time monitoring, data analytics, and communication technologies to tackle modern urban issues like traffic jams, pollution, and changing mobility requirements.

A linked solution such as a smart public transportation system makes traveling easy and convenient for passengers. Smart bus stops, smart public buses, cloud computing, 5G, and remote users via mobile or online applications are the key components of a smart public transit system.

### 8.1.1. **Transit Management System:**

8.1.1.1. **Smart Traffic Management:** Centralized traffic management systems enable transit authorities to intelligently manage public transportation routes, cameras, traffic lights, and emergency routing as cities become smarter. This helps optimize traffic flow and enhance overall efficiency.

8.1.1.2. **5G networks with the Internet of Things:** Quick connectivity for large-scale data streams is made possible by the growing availability of 5G networks. When combined with the Internet of Things (IoT), transit agencies may gather and track data from a variety of devices at a reasonable cost, which improves operational efficiency and decision-making.

8.1.1.3.    **Safety and Rider Experience:** In order to improve both safety and the aboard experience, aging transit systems are looking to update. By addressing these issues, new technologies can guarantee a more secure and pleasurable travel experience for travelers.

Thus, smart transit systems are transforming urban mobility by utilizing technology to develop public transportation options that are more effective, dependable, and sustainable.

8.1.2.  **Public Transportation Systems Components:**

8.1.2.1.    **Intelligent Transportation Systems (ITS):**

- **Real-time Monitoring and Control:** Public transportation vehicles are tracked in real-time using GPS, sensors, and Internet of Things devices. As a result, routes can be optimized and waiting times can be decreased through dynamic scheduling and dispatching.
- **Traffic Management:** Transit vehicles can have their traffic signals and flow prioritized in real-time, which will cut down on delays and increase timeliness.

8.1.2.2.    **Data Analytics:**

- **Predictive Analytics** analyzes historical and current data to forecast demand trends, improve scheduling, and effectively distribute resources.
- **Passenger Flow Analysis:** Better service planning is made possible by big data's ability to comprehend passenger behavior, peak usage periods, and well-traveled routes.

8.1.2.3.    **Smart Ticketing Platforms:**

- **Contactless Payments**: By facilitating smooth, cashless transactions, wearable technology, smartphone apps, and smart cards shorten boarding times and enhance user satisfaction.
- **Integrated Fare Systems:** Integrated ticketing systems for buses, trains, and bicycles make transfers simple and improve convenience all around.

8.1.2.4.    **Information Systems for Passengers:**

- **Real-time Updates:** Passengers can get real-time updates on arrival times, delays, and other routes via digital displays, smartphone apps, and SMS services.

- **Personalized Services:** Considering user preferences and current conditions, apps can provide personalized trip planning.

### 8.1.2.5. Electric and Self-Driving Cars:

- **Autonomous Transit:** With cutting-edge sensors and artificial intelligence (AI), self-driving buses and shuttles can operate in a safe manner, save labor expenses, and offer dependable service.
- **Electric and Hybrid Vehicles**: Using electric buses helps to preserve the environment by cutting emissions and operating expenses.

## 8.1.3. Advantages of Smart Public Transport Systems:

### 8.1.3.1. Reliability and Efficiency:

- Reduced travel times and improved service dependability are the results of improved route optimization and real-time modifications.
- Service interruptions and downtime are decreased with predictive maintenance for infrastructure and automobiles.

### 8.1.3.2. User Experience:

- Enhanced accessibility with simple payment options and real-time information.
- Improved service predictability and shorter wait times boost customer satisfaction.

### 8.1.3.3. Environmental Impact:

- Reduced carbon footprint by using electric vehicles, improving traffic management, and designing routes more efficiently.
- Choosing public transportation over private automobiles helps reduce air pollution in cities.

### 8.1.3.4. Financial Benefits:

- Effective public transportation networks draw in business and strengthen regional economies.
- All things considered, productivity is increased by less traffic and quicker commutes.

### 8.1.3.5. Social Inclusion:

- Enhanced transit accessibility for neglected areas.
- Increased choices for low-income, senior, and disabled communities to get around.

## 8.1.4. Challenges and Considerations

### 8.1.4.1. Implementation Costs:

- High upfront costs for technology, infrastructure, and training.
- Financing for renovations and long-term upkeep must be consistent.

### 8.1.4.2. Data Security and Privacy:

- Safeguarding system security against cyberattacks and protecting passenger data privacy.
- Observing data protection laws and upholding public confidence.

### 8.1.4.3. Interoperability:

- It can be difficult to integrate diverse systems and technologies from different manufacturers.
- Ensuring interoperability and smooth functioning across various transportation modalities.

### 8.1.4.4. Regulatory and Policy Framework:

- Establishing laws and policies that will encourage the use of smart transit technologies.
- Coordination between various public and private organizations.

### 8.1.5. Case Studies:

### 8.1.5.1. Singapore:

- Contactless payments, real-time passenger information, and smart traffic lights are all part of the extensive Intelligent Transportation System (ITS) that Singapore's Land Transport Authority (LTA) has put in place.
- The city-state's use of predictive modeling and data analytics has greatly increased transit efficiency and decreased traffic.

### 8.1.5.2. London:

- For buses, trains, and the subterranean system, Transport for London (TfL) uses a single fare system (Oyster card and contactless payments).
- Through smartphone apps and digital displays, real-time updates and arrival information are readily accessible.

### 8.1.5.3. Brazil's Curitiba:

- Curitiba, which is renowned for creating the first Bus Rapid Transit (BRT) system, has incorporated smart technologies to improve the efficiency and dependability of its services.
- The city optimizes routes and controls bus frequencies using real-time data.

### 8.1.6. A Look at the Future:

**8.1.6.1.   Integration with Smart City Projects**:

- Smart public transportation networks are essential components of larger smart city frameworks, improving the general sustainability and livability of urban areas.
- Cooperation with waste management systems, electricity grids, and smart buildings, among other elements of smart cities.

**8.1.6.2.   Creative Mobility Solutions:**

- Incorporating new modes of transportation into the public transportation system, such as micro-mobility, bike sharing, and ride-sharing.
- Creation of platforms for mobility-as-a-service (MaaS) that include complete trip planning and payment options.

**8.1.6.3.   Cutting-edge Technologies:**

- Ongoing research into blockchain, AI, and machine learning to improve security and operational effectiveness.
- Expansion of driverless car testing and use in public transportation systems.

In summary, the goal of smart public transportation systems is to develop transportation networks that are more sustainable, user-friendly, and efficient by combining IT and urban design. Even though they present certain difficulties, improved mobility, environmental sustainability, and economic dynamism make them an essential part of contemporary urban development. Urban transit is expected to change as a result of these systems' continuous development, strengthening urban connectivity and resilience.

## 8.2.   The Rise of Autonomous Vehicles: Consequences for Information Technology and Urban Planning

With the advent of autonomous vehicles, the transportation sector is leading the way in a dramatic technological revolution. Due to its autonomous operation and reliance on cutting-edge technologies like artificial intelligence and sensors to negotiate roads and highways, these cars are completely changing the transportation industry. For the transportation sector to have a safer and more sustainable future, artificial intelligence (AI) technology must be included into autonomous driving.

From Level 0, when AI technology is not used in the car, to Level 5, where the AI system can drive autonomously even in unrestricted areas and with variable weather, autonomous vehicles have gone through several stages of development. The advantages of fully automated vehicles become clearer as we approach that goal.

With the use of cutting-edge technologies, *Autonomous Vehicles* (AVs) are completely changing the way people travel. These cars can navigate and function without the need for human interaction. Information technology (IT) and urban planning are both greatly impacted by this shift, which has wide-ranging effects on everything from infrastructure design and traffic management to economic models and regulatory frameworks.

8.2.1. **Technological Bases:**

8.2.1.1.    **Hardware and Sensors:**

    a. **Lidar and Radar:** These sensors offer a 360-degree perspective of the area around the car and can identify pedestrians, other cars, and obstructions.

    b. **Cameras:** For the purposes of object identification, traffic sign recognition, and lane detection, high-resolution cameras record visual data.

    c. **GPS and IMU:** Accurate localization and navigation are guaranteed by the *Global Positioning System* (GPS) and *Inertial Measurement Units* (IMU).

8.2.1.2.   **Algorithms and Software:**

    a. **Perception:** To perceive the surroundings, recognize things, anticipate motions, and comprehend road conditions, software analyzes data from sensors.

    b. **Making Plans and Decisions:** The optimal route for the car is chosen by algorithms that take into account dynamic barriers, traffic laws, and passenger safety.

    c. **Control:** Uses steering, braking, and acceleration adjustments to make sure the car stays on the intended course.

8.2.1.3.   **Connectivity:**

    a. **V2X Communication:** By allowing autonomous vehicles (AVs) to communicate with infrastructure (V2I), networks (V2N), and other vehicles (V2V), V2X communication improves situational awareness and coordination.

   b. **5G Networks**: Real-time data exchange is supported by high-speed, low-latency communication networks, which is essential for AV operations.

## 8.2.2. Consequences for Urban Planning:

### 8.2.2.1. Infrastructure Design:

   a. **Smart Roads:** AV navigation and data collecting are supported by the integration of sensors, cameras, and communication systems into the road infrastructure.

   b. **Dedicated Lanes**: AV lanes should be implemented to improve traffic flow.

   c. **Parking and Drop-off Zones:** Restructuring urban areas to make room for parking options tailored to AVs as well as convenient locations for drop-off and pick-up.

### 8.2.2.2. Traffic Management:

   a. **Dynamic Traffic Control**: Real-time traffic management systems that adjust traffic flow and signal timings in response to Autonomous Vehicles (AV) data, hence minimizing traffic and expediting travel times.

   b. **Platooning**: AVs can ride in "platoons," or closely spaced groups, which lowers aerodynamic drag and increases road capacity.

### 8.2.2.3. Zoning and Land Use:

   a. **Decreased Parking Demand:** By dropping off and parking in less crowded locations, AVs can free up urban property for other purposes, such as parks, business projects, or residential construction.

   b. **Mixed-Use Developments**: Promoting mixed-use projects with AV-based public transportation to lessen the need for lengthy trips.

### 8.2.2.4. Effect on the Environment:

   a. **Reduction of Emissions**: AVs, especially electric AVs, can drastically cut down on greenhouse gas emissions and air pollution in cities.

   b. **Effective route:** Fuel consumption is decreased and the environmental effect is minimized with optimized route.

## 8.2.3. Social and Economic Consequences:

### 8.2.3.1. Job Creation and Displacement:

a. **Employment Shift:** While AVs may eliminate jobs in driving and logistics, they also open up new possibilities in cybersecurity, technological development, and maintenance.

b. **Reskilling:** Programs to retrain employees for new positions in the AV ecosystem are known as reskilling.

**8.2.3.2. Fairness and Availability:**

a. **Inclusive Mobility**: AVs can improve mobility for people who are unable to use traditional forms of transportation, such as the elderly and the disabled.

b. **Affordability**: Users' transportation expenses can be lowered via pooled AV services and economies of scale.

**8.2.3.3. Security and Safety:**

a. **Decreased Accidents:** AVs may considerably lower the number of traffic accidents brought on by human mistake.

b. **Risks Associated with Cybersecurity:** putting strong defenses in place to keep AV systems safe from hacking and data breaches.

**8.2.4. Policy and Regulatory Aspects to Take into Account:**

**8.2.4.1. Testing and Safety Standards:**

a. **Regulatory Frameworks:** Creating thorough rules and guidelines for the installation, testing, and use of antivirus software.

b. **Testing Protocols:** Strict testing procedures are used to guarantee the security and dependability of AVs before they are widely used.

**8.2.4.2. Ethics and Data Privacy:**

a. **Data protection:** Rules to safeguard the confidentiality of user information gathered by antivirus software.

b. **Ethical Determination**: Handling moral conundrums in autonomous vehicle decision-making, including deciding whether level of importance to give pedestrian or passenger safety.

**8.2.4.3. Insurance and Liability:**

a. **Legal Liability:** Determining who is responsible for accidents involving autonomous vehicles (AVs)—software developers, manufacturers, or operators?

b. **Models of Insurance:** creating new insurance plans to account for the particular hazards connected to autonomous vehicles.

### 8.2.5. Real World Applications and Case Studies:

### 8.2.5.1. Waymo (USA):

- **Deployment:** Waymo, an Alphabet Inc. subsidiary, runs a commercial autonomous vehicle taxi service in Phoenix, Arizona.
- **Technology:** For safety and navigation, LIDAR, radar, cameras, and sophisticated AI algorithms are combined.

### 8.2.5.2. Nuro (USA):

- **Delivery Services:** Nuro partners with businesses such as Kroger and Domino's to provide autonomous delivery vans for groceries and small items.
- **Impact:** Lowers delivery expenses and improves customer convenience.

### 8.2.5.3. Baidu Apollo (China):

- **Open Platform**: Baidu's Apollo platform is an open-source AV development program that supports a variety of partners, including tech companies and automakers.
- **Pilot Initiatives:** extensive pilot projects that incorporate AVs into urban mobility systems in places like Changsha and Beijing.

### 8.2.6. A Look at the Future:

### 8.2.6.1. Integration with Smart Cities:

- Autonomous vehicles (AVs) play a crucial role in smart city projects, collaborating with other intelligent infrastructure to enhance urban living.
- Cooperation to create integrated mobility solutions across the public and private sectors.

### 8.2.6.2. Cutting-edge Technologies:

- Safety and capabilities of autonomous vehicles will be improved by ongoing developments in AI, machine learning, and sensor technologies.
- Investigation of quantum computing for on-the-spot processing and sophisticated environment decision-making.

### 8.2.6.3. Sustainable Mobility:

- A focus on shared and electric AVs to advance environmentally friendly urban transportation.
- AV integration with smart grids and renewable energy sources.

In summary, the emergence of self-driving cars offers a revolutionary chance for IT and urban design. Autonomous vehicles (AVs) have the potential to greatly improve mobility, lessen environmental impact, and build more livable cities through the integration of advanced technologies with creative urban planning. However, in order to guarantee that the advantages of AVs are widely shared, this shift calls for meticulous planning, strong regulatory frameworks, and an emphasis on equity and inclusivity. Urban environments will change as autonomous car technology continues to advance.

## 8.3. Intelligent Traffic Management: Integrating IT and Urban Planning

Most big cities, particularly those in emerging nations, struggle with traffic congestion. Queues, slower moving traffic, and longer travel times are all parts of traffic congestion. These factors wear down and stress out commuters, which lowers productivity and adds to intangible societal costs. In addition, a variety of other aspects are impacted, either directly or indirectly, including the utilization of natural resources, the surrounding area, commuter safety, etc.

As a result, every expanding metropolis faces the difficulty of traffic congestion. Due to a number of factors, building new roads is rarely profitable in light of the growing traffic. On the other hand, building more roads may exacerbate traffic congestion by increasing demand for motorized transportation and quickly using up the additional capacity. This is becoming more and more obvious as major cities experience traffic jams and delays. As a result, over time, a number of mitigating measures have been put into place.

By utilizing cutting-edge information technology, *Intelligent Traffic Management Systems (ITMS) maximize traffic flow, lessen congestion, and enhance urban mobility.* These systems improve the effectiveness and security of transportation networks by utilizing real-time data, predictive analytics, and automated control mechanisms. It is crucial for an IT and urban planning specialist to comprehend the elements, advantages, and implementation difficulties of ITMS.

### 8.3.1. **Important Parts of Intelligent Traffic Management Systems:**
#### 8.3.1.1. **Sensors and Data Collection:**
      a. **Traffic Cameras:** Record live video footage to keep an eye on accidents, infractions, and traffic movement.

b. **Inductive Loop Sensors** are used in roads to count traffic and detect the presence of vehicles.

c. **Lidar and Radar:** Monitor vehicle velocity and identify items in the road and surrounding areas.

d. Utilize **GPS and Mobile Data** to gather information about the position, speed, and travel habits of vehicles.

8.3.1.2. **Analytics and Data Processing:**

a. **Big Data Analytics:** Examine vast amounts of traffic data to spot trends, forecast bottlenecks, and make recommendations for enhancements.

b. **Machine Learning Algorithms:** Learn from real-time and historical data to improve predictive capabilities.

c. **Simulation Models:** To evaluate scenarios and design infrastructure changes, use traffic simulation software.

8.3.1.3. **Communication Networks:**

a. **Vehicle-to-Everything (V2X):** Facilitates communication between automobiles, networks, pedestrians, and infrastructure, improving coordination and situational awareness.

b. **5G Networks:** Ensure that there is fast, low-latency connectivity available for real-time control and data transmission.

8.3.1.4. **Control Systems:**

a. **Adaptive Traffic Signal Control** reduces waiting times and enhances flow by modifying signal timings in response to current traffic circumstances.

b. **Ramp metering:** To reduce traffic, it regulates how quickly cars get on roadways.

c. **Dynamic Lane Management:** This feature, which includes reversible lanes and dedicated bus or HOV lanes, modifies lane usage according to traffic demand.

8.3.1.5. **Information Exchange:**

a. **Variable Message Signs (VMS):** Give drivers up-to-date information on accidents, traffic patterns, and travel times.

b. **Navigation Systems and Mobile Applications:** Provide individualized traffic status updates and route recommendations.

c. **Campaigns for Public Information:** Inform the public about traffic control measures and encourage defensive driving.

8.3.2. **Advantages of Intelligent Traffic Management Systems:**

8.3.2.1. **Optimization of Traffic Flow:**

   a. **Decreased Congestion:** By adjusting traffic signals and lane usage in real-time, bottlenecks are avoided and traffic flows freely.

   b. **Better Travel Times:** Travel times are more predictable and shorter when traffic flow is optimized.

8.3.2.2. **Increased Security:**

   a. **Accident Reduction:** You can prevent accidents and lessen their severity by using real-time monitoring and quick incident response.

   b. **Pedestrian Safety:** Bicycle and pedestrian safety is increased with better crossing signals and V2X communication.

8.3.2.3. **Effect on the Environment:**

   a. **Decreased Emissions:** Fuel consumption and emissions are decreased by improved traffic flow and less congestion.

   b. **Encouragement of Sustainable Modes:** Giving non-motorized and public transportation priority encourages more environmentally friendly transportation options.

8.3.2.4. **Economic Benefits:**

   a. **Enhanced Productivity:** Shorter travel distances and reduced traffic result in more productivity, which boosts the economy.

   b. **Cost Savings:** Fuel expenses, vehicle wear and tear, and the requirement for large-scale infrastructure investments are all decreased by effective traffic management.

8.3.2.5. **User Experience:**

   a. **Increased Commuter Satisfaction:** Reliable travel schedules and less delays make commuters' experiences better all around.

   b. **Accessibility:** Residents and businesses can gain from better traffic management by having easier access to urban areas and amenities.

### 8.3.3. Implementation Difficulties:

### 8.3.3.1. Security and Privacy of Data:

   a. **Data protection:** It's critical to protect the privacy of information gathered from people and automobiles.

   b. **Cybersecurity:** To preserve system integrity and public confidence, traffic management systems must be shielded from cyberattacks.

### 8.3.3.2. Investment in Infrastructure:

    a. **High Initial Costs:** Installing sensors, communication networks, and control systems requires a large financial outlay.

    b. **Maintenance and Upgrades:** It is necessary to budget for ongoing expenses related to upkeep and modernization of infrastructure.

**8.3.3.3. Interoperability:**

    a. **System Integration:** It is difficult to make sure that diverse parts and technologies from different manufacturers interact harmoniously.

    b. **Standardization**: It is essential to create and follow industry standards for system interfaces, communication protocols, and data formats.

**8.3.3.4. Framework for Regulation and Policy:**

    a. **Supportive Regulations**: establishing legal structures to facilitate the implementation and management of ITMS.

    b. **Coordination:** Making certain that various governmental entities, local governments, and private players work together.

**8.3.3.5. Public Acceptance:**

    a. **User Adaptation** involves promoting the use of new technologies and educating the public about the advantages of ITMS.

    b. **Equity:** Making sure that traffic management strategies are fair and don't unfairly advantage or harm particular groups.

**8.3.4. Case Studies:**

**8.3.4.1. Singapore:**

- **Smart Mobility 2030:** The Expressway Monitoring and Advisory System (EMAS) and the Green Link Determining (GLIDE) system for adaptive traffic signal control are two of the many ITMSs that Singapore's Land Transport Authority (LTA) has put in place.
- **Results:** Significant improvements in safety and environmental advantages, as well as a reduction in traffic and travel times.

**8.3.4.2. London (UK):**

- **London Streets Traffic Control Centre (LSTCC):** Uses dynamic messaging systems and adaptive signal control to integrate data from many sources and manage traffic in real-time.
- **Results:** Better incident management, less traffic congestion, and improved traffic flow.

**8.3.4.3. Los Angeles (USA):**

- Traffic signal monitoring and control throughout the city is done by **Automated Traffic Surveillance and Control (ATSAC)**, which makes use of a network of sensors and cameras.
- **Results:** Decreased traffic, shorter travel times, and improved incident response capabilities.

### 8.3.5. A Look at the Future:

### 8.3.5.1.  Integration with Self-Driving Cars:

- AVs and ITMS coordination for improved safety and traffic flow.
- Creating V2X communication guidelines to improve compatibility.

### 8.3.5.2.  Initiatives for Smart Cities:

- Incorporating ITMS into larger frameworks for smart cities, such as those for public transportation, smart grids, and urban planning.
- utilizing IoT and AI to improve predictive analytics and decision-making in real-time.

### 8.3.5.3.  Sustainable Mobility:

- Encouraging the usage of electric cars (EVs) and fusing traffic management systems with the infrastructure needed for charging them.
- Promoting the use of multimodal transportation options to lessen dependency on personal vehicles.

### 8.3.5.4.  Cutting-Edge Technologies:

- Applying machine learning and artificial intelligence to more advanced traffic management and forecasting.
- Investigating the use of blockchain in ITMS transaction management and data exchange for transparent and safe practices.

In summary, intelligent traffic management systems, which offer significant advantages in terms of efficiency, safety, environmental effect, and user experience, constitute a crucial nexus between IT and urban planning. To face the problems of contemporary urban mobility, communities can modernize their transportation networks by utilizing data-driven methodologies and new technologies. But for implementation to be successful, data protection, infrastructure spending, interoperability, legal frameworks, and public acceptance must all be carefully considered. These systems will be crucial in determining how urban mobility and smart city development develop in the future as they continue to improve.

# Chapter 9: Smart Waste Management Solutions

## 9.1. Smart Waste Collection Systems

Utilizing technology, smart garbage collection systems maximize waste management by lowering expenses, increasing efficiency, and limiting negative environmental effects. Waste management is a major worldwide issue that calls for creative solutions to maximize resources and promote sustainability. Conventional methods frequently fall short of meeting the growing amount of waste and its impact on the environment. But there are encouraging new approaches to dealing with the complexity of waste management systems thanks to the development of artificial intelligence (AI) technologies.

This chapter offers a thorough analysis of artificial intelligence's contribution to trash management, including collection, sorting, recycling, and monitoring. It highlights the need for better data quality, privacy precautions, cost-effectiveness, and ethical issues while outlining the possible advantages and difficulties of each use. Advances in machine learning, potential futures for AI integration with the Internet of Things (IoT), and the significance of cooperative frameworks and policy initiatives were also covered. Here's a thorough examination of intelligent waste management systems:

### 9.1.1. **Important Components:**

9.1.1.1. **Sensors:** These sensors, which are installed in waste bins, keep an eye on fill levels instantly. In addition to detecting when a bin is empty, almost full, or full, certain sophisticated sensors can also determine what kind of waste is in the bin.

9.1.1.2. **Connectivity:** The sensors send data to a central system via a variety of communication methods, including as cellular networks, LPWAN, and the Internet of Things. This guarantees remote monitoring and real-time data flow.

9.1.1.3. **Data Analytics**: To forecast trends and improve collection routes, the gathered data is examined. Analytics can also be used to predict the patterns in waste output in the future.

9.1.1.4. **Route Optimization:** To find the most effective collection routes that minimize travel time, fuel consumption, and operating expenses, algorithms and artificial intelligence are utilized.

9.1.1.5. **User Interface:** To monitor bin statuses, modify routes, and access reports and analytics, waste management operators can make use of dashboards and mobile apps.

9.1.1.6. **Integration with Other Systems:** For a more comprehensive approach to urban management, smart garbage collection systems can be coupled with smart city platforms, environmental monitoring tools, and municipal systems.

9.1.2. **Advantages:**

9.1.2.1. **Cost Savings and Efficiency:** Optimised routes result in lower fuel consumption and labor expenses. Real-time data eliminates needless travel by enabling collecting just when needed.

9.1.2.2. **Environmental Impact:** Lower carbon footprints are a result of better routes, which reduce automobile emissions. More recycling and waste reduction are made possible by effective waste management techniques.

9.1.2.3. **Enhanced Service Quality:** By guaranteeing that bins are emptied prior to overflow, real-time monitoring enhances cleanliness and lowers hazards to the public's health.

9.1.2.4. **Data-Driven Decision Making:** By offering insights into waste generation trends, analytics assist municipalities in making more informed plans and putting into practice efficient waste management procedures.

9.1.2.5. **Scalability:** For all-encompassing urban management, systems can be connected with other smart city solutions or expanded to cover bigger areas.

9.1.3. **Challenges:**

9.1.3.1. **Initial Expenses:** Installing sensors and integrating them with current systems may be expensive.

9.1.3.2. **Maintenance:** Both routine upkeep and sporadic replacement are needed for sensors and communication devices.

9.1.3.3. **Data Security and Privacy:** It's critical to make sure that the information gathered is safe and used properly.

9.1.3.4. **Adoption and Training:** Change can be resisted, and municipal employees must receive training in order to operate and administer these systems.

9.1.4. **Examples of Smart Waste Collection System:**

   a. **Bigbelly:** Waste bins driven by solar energy that are fitted with sensor technology and compaction to lessen overflow and pickup frequency.

   b. **Enevo:** Offers wireless sensors and analytics to streamline the routes and timing of waste collection.

   c. **SmartBin:** IoT-based sensors and software for real-time tracking and route optimization are provided by SmartBin.

   d. **Rubicon:** Provides data analytics, integrates with fleets, and manages waste collection more effectively by using mobile apps and cloud-based solutions.

9.1.5. **Future Trends**

   a. **AI and Machine Learning:** Improved predictive analytics for more accurate waste generation predictions and flexible route planning.

   b. **Advanced Materials and Design:** Creation of more adaptable and robust sensors that are resistant to a range of environmental factors.

   c. **Integration with Circular Economy Models:** Enhanced data on waste streams enable more effective recycling and resource recovery.

   d. **Community Engagement:** Encouraging residents to participate in waste reduction initiatives by giving them information about their recycling and waste production practices through applications and platforms.

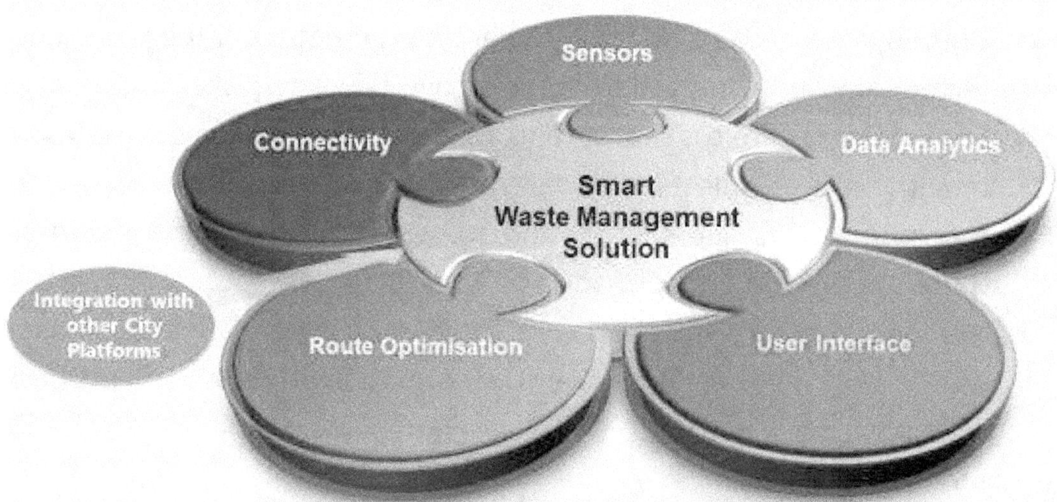


Source: Smart Cities: *The Technology Transforming Urban Living*, GoodMan Series, (Patrick Mukosha, 2024).

*Figure 6: Important Components of a Smart Waste Management Solution*

By utilizing technology to address the growing issues associated with garbage in urban areas, smart waste collection systems represent a big step towards more sustainable and effective urban waste management.

## 9.2. Waste-to-Energy Technologies

*Waste-to-Energy* (WtE) technologies are methods that transform waste into fuel, heat, or electricity, among other useful types of energy. These innovations contribute to lowering greenhouse gas emissions, decreasing the amount of garbage dumped in landfills, and offering a substitute energy source. Waste-to-Energy (WtE) technologies include a range of waste treatment procedures that transform waste materials into energy, either as heat or electricity. These systems are capable of processing a variety of waste materials, from liquid waste (like home sewage) to semi-solid wastes (like thickened sludge from effluent treatment plants). An outline of the main WtE technologies is provided below:

9.2.1. **Important Technologies:**

9.2.1.1.	**Incineration:** In this process, fuel obtained from garbage or municipal solid waste (MSW) is directly burned in the presence of oxygen at temperatures between 750 and 1100°C. In a boiler or steam turbine, it generates steam for the production of heat or power. Incineration can produce power and/or heat simultaneously.

    a. **Process:** High-temperature burning of garbage produces heat, which is subsequently utilized to create steam, which powers turbines to generate electricity.

    b. **Benefits:** Produces a large amount of energy and greatly reduces waste volume.

    c. **Challenges:** Ash disposal, emissions management, and public impression issues.

9.2.1.2. **Gasification:** In gasification, waste is partially oxidized between 800 and 1200°C in the presence of regulated oxygen. This includes wood waste, agricultural wastes, sewage sludge, and plastic trash. Syngas, which is created during this process, can be burned again or transformed into chemical feedstock.

    a. **Process:** Reacts organic compounds at high temperatures with a regulated quantity of oxygen to produce synthetic gas, or syngas. Electricity can be produced from the syngas.

    b. **Advantages:** Lower pollutants, more efficient than incineration, and capacity to manage a variety of waste types.

    c. **Challenges:** Include the necessity for waste pre-treatment, complicated technology, and a high initial expenditure.

9.2.1.3. **Pyrolysis:** Pyrolysis: In the absence of oxygen, waste (such as wood waste, agricultural wastes, sewage sludge, and plastic trash) is thermally broken down between 300 and 1300°C. It produces liquid fuel that can be burned or transformed into chemical feedstock.

    a. **Process:** Produces bio-oil, syngas, and char by breaking down organic waste materials at high temperatures without oxygen.

    b. **Benefits** include producing a number of beneficial byproducts, handling different waste kinds, and having comparatively low emissions.

    c. **Difficulties:** Needs careful condition management and by-product market development.

9.2.1.4. **Anaerobic Digestion:** In this process, easily broken down organic waste is biodegraded by anaerobic bacteria without the presence of oxygen. It can handle food waste, liquids and sludges, animal and human excreta, and organic parts of MSW. Biogas, which is utilized as fuel for power generation, and digestate are produced via anaerobic digestion.

    a. **Process:** Microorganisms break down organic waste (such as food and agricultural waste) in the absence of oxygen to produce digestate and biogas, primarily methane.

    b. **Benefits** include reducing organic waste, producing biogas, a renewable energy source, and producing nutrient-rich digestate that can be used as fertilizer.

    c. **Obstacles:** restricted to organic waste, necessitates cautious biological process management.

9.2.1.5. **Recovery of Landfill Gas:** The process of gathering, processing, and utilizing landfill gas (LFG) for cooking, space heating/cooling (absorption chillers), car fuel, or combustion to generate power is known as landfill gas recovery or utilization. A landfill will switch from aerobic to anaerobic digestion and begin producing LFG after around a year of operation.

    a. **Process:** Gathers methane gas from organic waste that is broken down anaerobically in landfills. After processing, the gas is extracted and used as a fuel source.

    b. **Advantages:** Lowers greenhouse gas emissions and makes use of garbage that is currently in landfills.

    c. **Challenges:** Long-term management is necessary; gas collection efficiency fluctuates.

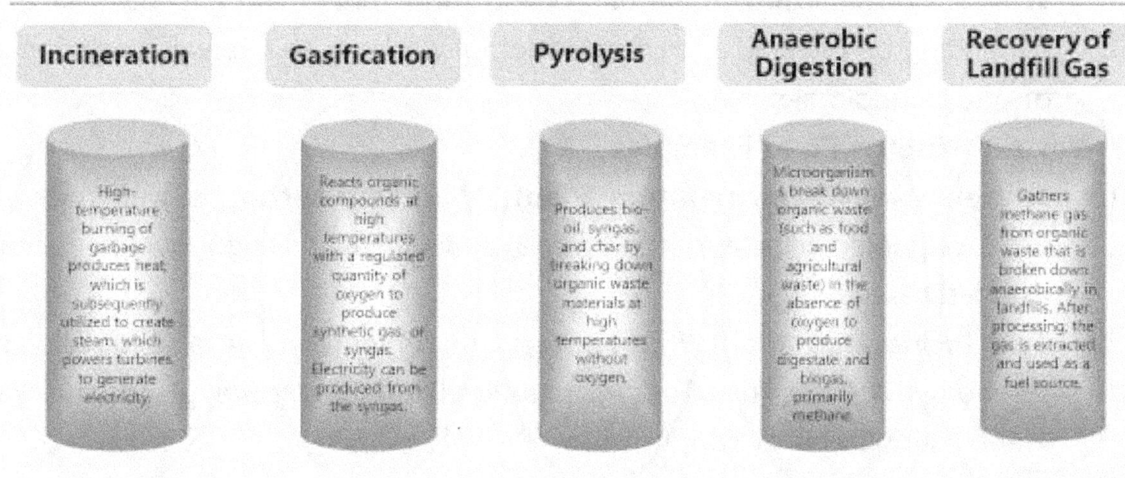


**Source:** Smart Cities: *The Technology Transforming Urban Living*, GoodMan Series, (Patrick Mukosha, 2024).

*Figure 7: Waste-to-Energy (WtE) Technologies*

These technologies meet the global requirement for sustainable energy while providing effective waste management. They offer potential solutions for both energy generation and waste management.

### 9.2.2. The Advantages of Energy-From-Waste Technologies

9.2.2.1. **Waste Volume Reduction:** Extends the life of landfills and lessens the demand for new landfills by drastically lowering the amount of waste that must be landfilled.

9.2.2.2. **Energy Production:** Offers a sustainable energy source, promoting energy security and diversification.

9.2.2.3. **Benefits**: Produces cleaner electricity than fossil fuels and lowers greenhouse gas emissions by keeping waste out of landfills.

9.2.2.4. **Economic Benefits:** Produces income from the development, upkeep, and operation of WtE facilities, and creates jobs in these areas.

### 9.2.3. Challenges and Considerations:

9.2.3.1. **Capital Costs:** The construction and upkeep of WtE facilities need a substantial upfront expenditure.

9.2.3.2. **Public Perception and Acceptance:** Opposition may arise because to worries about pollution, health effects, and aesthetics.

9.2.3.3.  **Emissions Control:** Making sure WtE plants adhere to strict environmental guidelines in order to reduce pollution.

9.2.3.4.  **Waste Composition:** Careful sorting and pre-treatment are necessary depending on the kind and composition of waste, as this can affect the efficacy of WtE technologies.

9.2.4.  **Waste-to-Energy Plant Examples**

9.2.4.1.  **Spittelau Waste Incineration Plant (Vienna, Austria)** is well-known for producing electricity and for having a distinctive design by Friedensreich Hundertwasser.

9.2.4.2.  **Tuas Incineration Plant (Singapore):** One of Southeast Asia's biggest waste-to-energy (WtE) facilities, Tuas Incineration Plant (Singapore) plays a major role in the nation's energy supply.

9.2.4.3.  **Tees Valley electricity-from-garbage Plant (UK)** converts garbage into electricity with the least amount of negative environmental impact possible by using cutting-edge gasification technology.

9.2.5.  **Future Trends:**

   a.  **Integration with Circular Economy:** WtE integration with other waste management and recycling initiatives will improve recycling and resource recovery. This is part of the circular economy integration.

   b.  **Technological Advancements** include improvements in efficiency and environmental performance through innovations in materials, process management, and emissions reduction.

   c.  **Policy and Regulation:** Encourage the development and implementation of WtE technologies via supportive policies and regulations.

   d.  **Public-Private Partnerships:** More cooperation between public and private sectors to finance, construct, and run WtE facilities.

Waste-to-Energy technologies are essential to sustainable waste management because they provide a workable answer to the problems associated with both producing energy and disposing of waste. We can progress towards a future that is more energy-efficient and sustainable by carrying out further research and development on these technologies.

Initiatives related to sustainability and recycling are essential for encouraging trash reduction, environmental preservation, and sustainable resource usage. These programs seek to establish a circular economy—one in which resources and goods are recycled, mended, and reused instead of being thrown away. An overview of numerous recycling and sustainability programs can be found here:

### 9.3.1.  **Important Recycling Projects:**

#### 9.3.1.1.  **Curbside Recycling:**

- **Description:** Programs managed by the local government that require citizens to separate recyclables (such as paper, plastic, glass, and metals) and put them in special bins for routine collection.
- **Benefits:** Include higher recycling rates, less waste going to landfills, and convenience for locals.
- **Obstacles:** Include high operating expenses, inconsistent participation rates, and recyclables contamination.

#### 9.3.1.2.  **Bottle Deposit Programs:**

- **Description:** Refunds are given to consumers who return beverage containers for recycling after they pay a deposit.
- **Benefits:** Include high can and bottle return rates, a decrease in litter, and encouragement of recycling.
- **Difficulties:** Infrastructure needed for redemption and collection; deposit amounts vary.

#### 9.3.1.3.  **Recycling of Electronic Waste (E-Waste)**

- **Description:** Programs for the safe recycling of electrical goods, including TVs, PCs, and cellphones.
- **Benefits:** Include reducing technological waste, recovering valuable materials, and keeping dangerous items out of landfills.
- **Challenges:** The logistics of data security, handling hazardous chemicals, and collection pose challenges.

#### 9.3.1.4.  **Initiatives for Recycling Plastic**

- **Description:** The endeavor to gather and reuse plastic items, such as packaging and single-use plastics.

- **Benefits:** Can produce new goods, preserve resources, and lessen pollution from plastic.
- **Challenges:** The challenges include contamination, economic viability, and the complexity of separating various types of plastics.

### 9.3.1.5. Neighborhood Recycling Facilities

- **Description:** Local locations where people can dispose of recyclables, frequently include goods like batteries and textiles that aren't picked up at the curb.
- **Benefits**: Include educating the public, encouraging community involvement, and offering recycling choices for a variety of items.
- **Challenges:** The difficulties lie in personnel, funding, and guaranteeing regular use.

## 9.3.2. Important Sustainability Projects

### 9.3.2.1. Zero Waste Programs:

- **Description:** Initiatives to reduce, reuse, and recycle all resources in an effort to eradicate waste.
- **Benefits:** Saves resources, encourages sustainable consumption, and lessens environmental effect.
- **Challenges:** Necessitates a substantial shift in behavior, infrastructure, and community involvement.

### 9.3.2.2. Eco-Friendly Packaging

- **Description:** The creation and application of recyclable, biodegradable, or renewable resource-based packaging materials.
- **Benefits**: Include a decrease in waste, resource conservation, and carbon impact.
- **Difficulties:** Price, effectiveness in comparison to conventional packaging, and customer acceptability.

### 9.3.2.3. Green Building Guidelines

- **Description:** Programs for certification (such as LEED and BREEAM) that encourage the construction of energy-efficient and ecologically friendly buildings.
- **Benefits:** Promotes healthier living conditions, decreases running expenses, and uses less energy.
- **Difficulties:** Increasing initial expenditures, intricate standards compliance, and continuous upkeep.

### 9.3.2.4. Initiatives for Corporate Sustainability

- **Description:** Programs that businesses have put in place to lessen their influence on the environment include waste management, energy conservation, and sustainable sourcing.
- **Benefits:** Complies with rules, lowers costs, and improves corporate image.
- **Challenges:** The initial investment, impact measurement, and incorporating sustainability into fundamental business operations are the challenges.

### 9.3.2.5. Sustainable Agriculture:

- **Description:** Crop rotation, organic farming, and less pesticide use are examples of farming practices that support social fairness, economic viability, and environmental health.
- **Benefits**: Include lowering chemical runoff, enhancing soil health, and conserving water.
- **Obstacles**: Include farmer transition costs, market demand, and certification procedures.

### 9.3.3. Instances of Successful Projects

### 9.3.3.1. Zero Waste Program (San Francisco):

- **Description:** The objective is to attain zero waste status by 2020 by implementing extensive recycling and composting initiatives.
- **Results**: Include high rates of landfill diversion, extensive community involvement, and creative policy.

### 9.3.3.2. Green Dot System (Germany):

- **Description:** In order to incentivize producers to reduce waste, they pay for packaging waste based on the quantity and kind of packaging they use.
- **Results:** increased package waste reduction, high recycling rates, and a move toward more environmentally friendly packaging materials.

### 9.3.3.3. The Worn Wear Program (Patagonia):

- **Description:** Promotes the repair, recycling, and repurposing of Patagonia products by its patrons.
- **Results:** Increases product longevity, lowers waste, and fosters a sustainable culture.

### 9.3.3.4. TerraCycle's Loop Initiative

- **Description:** Collaborates with well-known brands to provide goods in reusable packaging that customers can return to be cleaned and refilled.
- **Results:** Encourages reuse, cuts down on single-use packaging, and gets customers involved in environmental initiatives.

### 9.3.4. Future Trends:

**9.3.4.1. Development of the Circular Economy:** In order to reduce waste and resource extraction, systems where materials are continuously reused and recycled should be prioritized.

**9.3.4.2. Technological Developments in Recycling:** Creation of recycling technologies that are more effective and efficient, such as sophisticated sorting systems and chemical recycling for plastics.

**9.3.4.3. Enhanced Regulatory Assistance:** Governments enacting tougher rules and incentives—like extended producer responsibility (EPR) laws—to encourage recycling and sustainability.

**9.3.4.4. Education and Involvement of Consumers:** A stronger focus on informing customers about the value of sustainability and recycling in order to promote responsible consumption habits.

To create a more sustainable future, recycling and sustainability measures are crucial. We can greatly lessen our influence on the environment and advance a healthier planet if we keep coming up with new ideas and growing these programs

# Chapter 10: Enhancing Public Safety and Security

## 10.1. Smart Surveillance Systems

By utilizing cutting-edge technologies, *smart surveillance systems can outperform conventional surveillance and offer more security, effectiveness, and situational awareness.* Cameras, sensors, artificial intelligence (AI), and data analytics are just a few of the components that these systems incorporate to provide more advanced monitoring and reaction mechanisms. This is a synopsis of intelligent monitoring systems:

### 10.1.1. **Important Elements:**

#### 10.1.1.1. **High-Resolution Cameras:**

- **Description:** High-definition (HD) and ultra-high-definition (UHD) security cameras are available nowadays, allowing them to capture comprehensive photos and videos.
- **Benefits** include sharper photos, enhanced identification skills, and better face and license plate recognition.

#### 10.1.1.2. **Machine Learning (ML) And Artificial Intelligence (AI)**

- **Description:** Real-time video feeds are analyzed by AI and ML algorithms to follow movements, identify objects, identify faces, and detect anomalies.
- **Benefits** include improved situational awareness, fewer false alarms, and automated threat identification.

#### 10.1.1.3. **Internet of Things (IoT) Sensors**

- **Description:** The integration of IoT sensors, such as environmental sensors, motion detectors, and temperature sensors, with cameras yields supplementary information and initiates alarms.
- **Benefits** include increased accuracy of surveillance, better context for notifications, and multifaceted monitoring.

#### 10.1.1.4. **Edge Computing**

- **Description:** Relying less on centralized servers and more on locally processing data on devices (at the edge).
- **Benefits** include lower latency, quicker reaction times, and less bandwidth use.

#### 10.1.1.5. **Cloud Computing:**

- **Description:** The cloud is used to store and process surveillance data for scalable management, storage, and analysis.
- **Benefits** include integration with other cloud-based services, scalability, and remote access.

10.1.1.6. **Data Analysis:**

- **Description:** The task involves examining substantial amounts of data from surveillance feeds in order to derive relevant patterns and insights.
- **Advantages** include enhanced decision-making, proactive security measures, and the ability to spot trends and abnormalities.

10.1.1.7. **Integration with Various Systems:**

- **Description:** Integrating alarm systems, access control, and other security infrastructure with surveillance systems.
- **Benefits**: Coordinated reactions, streamlined operations, and comprehensive security management.

10.1.2. **Advantages of Smart Surveillance Systems:**

10.1.2.1. **Enhanced Safety**

- **Real-Time Monitoring** is ongoing observation combined with prompt alerting and reaction.
- **Proactive Threat Detection**: Artificial intelligence (AI)-powered analysis can spot possible dangers before they get worse.

10.1.2.2. **Efficiency of Operations**

- **Automated Processes:** Free up security staff to concentrate on other important duties by reducing the requirement for continual human monitoring.
- **Resource Optimization:** Uses data-driven insights to distribute security resources in an efficient manner.

10.1.2.3. **Enhanced Accuracy:**

- **Diminished False Alarms:** Sophisticated analytics distinguish between genuine dangers and harmless actions.
- **Improved Identification:** Accurate identification is enhanced by high-resolution images and facial recognition.

10.1.2.4. **Flexibility and Scalability**

- **Expandable Systems:** Easily expandable to accommodate more facilities or greater regions.

- **Remote Access:** Systems based on the cloud enable control and monitoring from any place.

10.1.2.5. **Data Application**

- **Historical Analysis:** To better understand prior incidents and future security initiatives, surveillance footage archives can be examined.
- **Predictive Analytics** uses patterns and trends to foresee possible security problems.

10.1.3. **Challenges and Considerations:**

10.1.3.1. **Privacy Concerns:**

- **Data Security** is the process of making sure that surveillance data is transferred and stored securely to thwart unwanted access.
- **Regulatory Compliance:** Following the rules and laws pertaining to privacy that control monitoring activities.

10.1.3.2. **Price:**

- **Initial Investment:** High initial expenditures are associated with sophisticated cameras, sensors, and computer equipment.
- **Updating and Maintenance**: Constant expenditures for hardware replacement, software upgrades, and system upkeep.

10.1.3.3. **Complexity:**

- **System Integration:** It might be difficult to integrate different components and make sure they function as a whole.
- **Technical Expertise:** To handle and run cutting-edge surveillance systems, qualified staff is needed.

10.1.3.4. **Data Management:**

- **Volume of Data:** Managing and archiving substantial amounts of sensor and high-resolution video data.
- **Analysis and Action:** Conducting effective data analysis and acting appropriately in response to revelations.

10.1.4. **Smart Surveillance System Examples**

10.1.4.1. **Ring of Steel (London):**

- **Description:** A central London network of automated number plate recognition (ANPR) equipment and security cameras.
- **Features** include interaction with law enforcement databases, real-time monitoring, and high-resolution cameras.

10.1.4.2. **Smart Nation Initiative (Singapore):**

- **Description:** The implementation of intelligent monitoring across the country is a component of a larger smart city project. **Features:** IoT integration, AI-powered analytics, and extensive urban surveillance.

**10.1.4.3. Domain Awareness System (DAS), (New York City):**

- **Description:** A comprehensive monitoring system encompassing cameras, sensors, and data analytics for the entire city.
- **Features**: Include predictive analytics, data fusion from many sources, and real-time crime detection.

**10.1.5. Upcoming Patterns**

**10.1.5.1. Advances in AI and Deep Learning**

- **Enhanced Algorithms**: To recognize objects and behaviors more accurately.
- **Improved Forecasting Skills**: For proactive security precautions.

**10.1.5.2. 5G Connectivity:**

- **Faster Data Transfer**: Makes it possible to stream high-definition video in real time and respond quickly.
- **Improved Connectivity**: To enable a wider use of IoT sensors.

**10.1.5.3. Improved Data Security and Privacy:**

- Creation of *access control and data encryption techniques* that are more secure.
- Application of technology like federated learning that protect privacy.

**10.1.5.4. Connectivity to the Infrastructure of Smart Cities**

- Smooth interaction with other smart city systems, such as public safety and traffic management.
- Enhanced living conditions for citizens and holistic urban management.

Smart surveillance systems, which provide reliable and effective answers to contemporary security challenges, mark a substantial breakthrough in security technology. As these systems develop further and become more integrated into larger technological ecosystems, they will be essential in improving security and safety in a variety of settings.

## 10.2. Emergency Response and Disaster Management

Coordination and execution of plans and actions to prevent, prepare for, respond to, and recover from natural or man-made disasters are key components of emergency response and disaster management. Resilience is increased and the impact of disasters is reduced via the use of technology, planning, and community involvement in effective systems.

10.2.1. **Essential Elements:**

10.2.1.1. **Early Warning Systems:**

- **Description:** Technologies and procedures that deliver precise and timely information on approaching natural disasters (such as hurricanes, tsunamis, and earthquakes) are described.
- **Benefits:** Reduces fatalities, permits early planning, and facilitates prompt evacuations.
- **Challenges:** Needs dependable data sources, advanced technology, and efficient lines of communication.

10.2.1.2. **Communication Networks:**

- **Description:** Strong and redundant communication networks that guarantee constant information flow in the lead-up to, during, and following a disaster.
- **Benefits:** Promotes real-time decision-making, information dissemination to the public, and agency coordination.
- **Challenges:** The challenges include ensuring access for all populations, repairing infrastructure, and resolving interoperability concerns.

10.2.1.3. **Incident Command Systems (ICS):**

- **Description:** The proposed method is a standardized strategy that integrates individuals, equipment, processes, and facilities to manage, coordinate, and regulate emergency response.
- **Benefits:** Ensures effective response operations, strengthens organizational structure, and enhances resource management.
- **Challenges:** Needs coordination across several agencies, roles and responsibilities that are defined, and training.

10.2.1.4. **Geospatial Information Systems (GIS):**

- **Description:** Tools for geographic data analysis and visualization to aid in disaster management decision-making are described.
- **Benefits** include enhancing situational awareness, supporting resource allocation, and identifying susceptible locations.
- **Challenges:** The challenges are assuring responders' accessibility, integrating with other systems, and ensuring data veracity.

10.2.1.5. **Social Media and Mobile Applications**

- **Description:** Platforms for information dissemination, alerting, and public-responder communication facilitation.
- **Benefits** include interactive communication, wide dissemination, and real-time updates.
- **Challenges:** include handling massive amounts of data, disparate access to technology, and misinformation.

10.2.1.6. **Emergency Operations Centers (EOCs)**

- **Description:** Centralized facilities for managing and coordinating emergency response.
- **Advantages:** Facilitates decision-making, improves cooperation, and streamlines communication.
- **Challenges:** Requires a strong infrastructure, is resource-intensive, and must run continuously.

10.2.2. **Advantages of Sophisticated Disaster Management and Emergency Response Systems**

10.2.2.1. **Enhanced Adaptability**

- **Increased Preparedness** by preparation, training, and role-playing.
- **Adaptability:** The capacity to react skillfully to a range of calamities.

10.2.2.2. **Diminished Effect**

- **Reduced Casualties**: Life is saved by prompt alerts and effective evacuations.
- **Property Protection**: Improving preparation and acting quickly lessen the chance of infrastructure damage.

10.2.2.3. **Enhanced Coordination**

- **Interagency Cooperation:** Responders work together more effectively when there is defined protocol and efficient communication.
- **Resource Optimization** is the effective distribution and application of resources in times of crisis.

10.2.2.4. **Increased Public Safety**

- **Information Dissemination:** Timely and accurate information enables the public to respond accordingly.
- **Community Involvement:** Including local communities in emergency planning and response initiatives fosters collaboration and mutual trust.

10.2.3. **Challenges and Considerations**

### 10.2.3.1. Vulnerability of Infrastructure

- **Deterioration of Transport and Communication Networks**: Unexpected events have the potential to destroy vital infrastructure, impeding rescue operations.
- **Redundancy and Backup Plans:** Making sure backup plans are set up to keep things running smoothly.

### 10.2.3.2. Data Management:

- **Reliability and Accuracy:** Ensuring the timely and accurate use of data in decision-making processes.
- **Integration:** The process of combining data for a thorough study from multiple sources.

### 10.2.3.3. Training and Readiness

- **Continuous Training**: Frequent drills and activities for the general public and responders.
- **Public Awareness**: ongoing community involvement and education.

### 10.2.3.4. Resources and Funding

- **Sustained Investment**: Making certain that programs for disaster preparedness and response receive regular support.
- **Resource Allocation:** Distributing resources among phases of readiness, reaction, and recuperation.

### 10.2.4. Case Studies: Effective Emergency Response and Disaster Management

### 10.2.4.1. Earthquake Early Warning System (Japan):

- **Description:** An earthquake early warning system that is available across the country.
- **Features:** Notifies authorities and locals of impending earthquakes by using a network of seismic sensors to identify the first waves of the event.
- **Results:** Allows for prompt preparations and evacuations, greatly lowering the number of fatalities and damage.

### 10.2.4.2. FEMA's National Incident Management System (NIMS) in USA:

- **Description:** A unified framework for handling all kinds of risks is described.
- **Features:** Gives incident management a standard vocabulary and framework.
- **Results:** Increases response efficiency through better collaboration between federal, state, and local entities.

**10.2.4.3. India's Cyclone Phailin Response:**

- **Description:** Detailed preparation and evacuation plan for Cyclone Phailin in 2013.
- **Features** include resource prepositioning, mass evacuations, and early warnings.
- **Results:** Minimized damage and casualties successfully, proving the value of integrated disaster management.

**10.2.5.      Future Trends:**

**10.2.5.1. Machine Learning and Artificial Intelligence**

- **Predictive Analytics** is the application of AI to forecast the effects of disasters and enhance reaction plans.
- **Automation:** Putting in place automated mechanisms to analyze data and make decisions in real time.

**10.2.5.2. Robotics and Drones**

- **Surveillance Assessment:** Drones are used for airborne monitoring and damage assessment in surveillance and evaluation.
- **Delivery:** Using robots and drones to transport goods and support rescue efforts.

**10.2.5.3. Integration of Smart Cities**

- **IoT and Sensors:** Linking disaster management systems with smart city infrastructure to provide real-time monitoring and reaction.
- **Urban Planning:** Creating disaster-resilient cities with integrated disaster management systems.

**10.2.5.4. Blockchain Technology**

- **Safe Data Sharing**: Enabling transparent and safe information exchange between authorities via blockchain technology.
- **Resource Management:** Blockchain technology improves supply chain and logistical operations.

For the purpose of preserving life and property, emergency response and disaster management are essential. Effective response to and recovery from disasters can be bolstered by utilizing cutting-edge technologies, enhancing coordination, and encouraging community involvement.

Using digital platforms and contemporary tools, community policing with technology improves communication between law enforcement and the communities they serve. The objectives of this strategy are to increase public safety, foster trust, and develop more transparent and responsive police services. An outline of how technology is used in community policing is provided below:

10.3.1. **Important Technologies:**
10.3.1.1. **Body-Worn Cameras (BWCs):**
- **Description:** Police officers' cameras are worn to capture their encounters with the public.
- **Benefits:** May enhance officer behaviours, strengthen accountability and transparency, and supply evidence for investigations.
- **Challenges:** Data management and storage, privacy issues, and the requirement for explicit usage guidelines.

10.3.1.2. **Mobile Applications:**
- **Description:** The applications enable locals to report crimes, provide tips, and get law enforcement alerts.
- **Benefits:** Promotes open dialogue between the public and law enforcement, boosts community involvement, and offers real-time information.
- **Challenges:** The challenges include managing app maintenance, protecting user privacy, and promoting broad adoption.

10.3.1.3. **Social Media Platforms:**
- **Description:** Sharing content, interacting with the community, and getting comments via social media sites like Facebook, Twitter, and Instagram.
- **Benefits:** Facilitates quick information dissemination, encourages transparency, and improves communication.
- **Challenges:** Misinformation, handling criticisms from the public, and maintaining regular updates are challenges.

10.3.1.4. **Geospatial Information Systems (GIS):**
- **Description:** Systems that map crime trends, distribute resources, and organize responses using spatial data analysis and visualization.

- **Advantages:** Facilitates data-driven decision-making, strengthens strategic planning, and raises situational awareness.
- **Challenges:** The challenges include data accuracy, system integration, and staff training on GIS usage.

10.3.1.5. **Plates Automated License Plate Recognition (ALPR)**

- **Description:** This technology takes license plate numbers and analyzes them using cameras.
- **Benefits:** Assists in monitoring traffic infractions, locating wanted criminals, and tracing stolen automobiles.
- **Difficulties:** Data management, privacy issues, and misuse possibility.

10.3.1.6. **Machine Learning (ML) And Artificial Intelligence (AI)**

- **Description:** Large datasets are analyzed by AI and ML algorithms to anticipate crime trends, locate hotspots, and assist with investigative tasks.
- **Benefits** include better resource allocation, proactive crime prevention, and enhanced predictive policing.
- **Challenges:** The challenges in implementing AI decision-making include potential biases in algorithms, ethical considerations, and maintaining openness.

10.3.2. **Technology-Enhanced Community Policing Benefits**

10.3.2.1. **Enhanced Trust and Transparency**

- **Accountability:** Social media and BWCs are two technologies that increase police activity transparency.
- **Engagement:** Open and honest communication with the community is fostered by social media and mobile apps.

10.3.2.2. **Better Reaction and Prevention to Crime**

- **Real-Time Data:** Resolving issues more quickly is made possible by having access to real-time information.
- **Predictive Analytics:** By examining patterns and trends, AI and ML assist in the prediction and prevention of crime.

10.3.2.3. **Enhanced Community Involvement:**

- **Reporting and comments:** Social media and mobile apps make it simple for locals to report problems and offer comments.
- **Collaborative Efforts:** GIS and community forums facilitate police and resident problem-solving together.

10.3.2.4. **Effective Resources Allocation:**

- **Data-Driven Decisions:** Predictive analysis of crime data, along with GIS and AI, enable the effective deployment of resources.
- **Operational Efficiency**: Officers can spend more time engaging with the community since automated solutions like ALPR streamline operations.

10.3.3. **Challenges and Considerations:**

10.3.3.1. **Data Security and Privacy:**

- **Data Protection** is the process of making sure that personal information gathered via different technologies is safe and appropriately used.
- **Legal Compliance:** Following the applicable laws and rules pertaining to data protection and surveillance.

10.3.3.2. **Trust and Public Perception:**

- **Transparency:** Making sure the public is aware of the usage of technologies and getting their support.
- **Handling Concerns:** Taking proactive measures to resolve worries over data usage and surveillance.

10.3.3.3. **Training and Adjustment**

- **Skills development:** Continual training is necessary to help officers acquire the skills they need to use new technologies efficiently.
- **Procedure Adaptation:** Keeping rules and guidelines current to allow technology to be easily incorporated into day-to-day activities.

10.3.3.4. **Infrastructure and Cost**

- **Finances:** Obtaining sufficient funds to buy, maintain, and upgrade technology.
- **Infrastructure:** Ensuring that the technical framework is in place to allow for optimal performance.

10.3.4. **Instances of Community Policing Enhanced by Technology**

10.3.4.1. **Seattle Police Department's Body-Worn Camera Program**

- **Description:** Using BWCs will improve accountability and transparency.
- **Results:** increased officer training, useful evidence for investigations, and increased community trust.

10.3.4.2. **COMPSTAT System (New York City):**

- **Description:** This system uses Geographic Information Systems (GIS) to track and analyze crime statistics.

- **Results:** decreased crime rates, better resource distribution, and data-driven policing tactics.

10.3.4.3. **Community Online Reporting Service (CORS), (Los Angeles Police Department):**
- **Description:** An online reporting portal that allows locals to report situations that are not emergencies.
- **Results:** Less work for officers, better management of non-emergency reports, and increased community involvement.

10.3.5. **Future Trends:**

10.3.5.1. **Sophisticated Analytics and AI**
- **Improved Proactive Policing:** Including more precise forecasts of crime trends are features of enhanced predictive policing.
- **Behavioral Analysis:** AI that scans for suspicious activity by examining body language and other indicators.

10.3.5.2. **Integration of the Internet of Things (IoT)**
- **Smart City Collaboration**: Integrating comprehensive urban safety management with smart city infrastructure.
- **Real-Time Monitoring:** IoT devices continuously gather data so that quick decisions and actions can be taken.

10.3.5.3. **Augmented Reality (AR) and Virtual Reality (VR)**
- **Training Simulations:** Virtual reality provides cops with immersive training sessions.
- **Enhanced Patrols:** AR gives police on patrol access to real-time information.

10.3.5.4. **Blockchain Technology for Data Protection**
- **Safe Documentation**: Employing blockchain technology to protect data and proof.
- **Transparent Transactions**: Making sure that data exchange and transactions are honest and transparent.

Through the use of technology in community policing, law enforcement and the community may collaborate more successfully. Police can improve their abilities, foster trust, and guarantee safer communities by utilizing contemporary technologies.

# Chapter 11: Advancements in Smart Healthcare

## 11.1. Telemedicine and Remote Health Monitoring

The fields of IT and urban planning are revolutionized by telemedicine and remote health monitoring, which offer significant advantages for the delivery of healthcare, especially in metropolitan areas. *These technologies improve public health management overall as well as accessibility and efficiency.* Here is a thorough explanation of each, backed up with examples:

11.1.1. **Telemedicine:** Is the practice of providing medical care from a distance by means of telecommunications technology. It includes a variety of services like electronic prescriptions, remote tests, and virtual consultations.

11.1.2. **Important Elements:**

1. **Virtual Consultations:**
   - By using video calls, patients can consult with medical professionals without having to physically visit them. This is especially helpful in cities where long travel times and heavy traffic can be major obstacles.
   - **Example:** The use of telemedicine increased dramatically in many cities during the COVID-19 pandemic. For example, in order to control the patient load and reduce the risk of viral transmission, New York City deployed a large number of telehealth services.

2. **Remote Diagnostics:**
   - With the use of sophisticated diagnostic instruments and software, medical professionals can examine patient data remotely and render precise diagnoses.
   - **Example:** Tele-ICUs, in which intensivists use real-time data and video feeds to remotely monitor and manage ICU patients in other hospitals.

3. **Electronic Prescriptions:**
   - Physicians can electronically email prescriptions to pharmacies for patients to pick up or have delivered.

- **Example:** In the UK, prescriptions can be electronically transferred from the doctor to the pharmacist through the NHS Electronic Prescription Service (EPS).

4. **Advantages:**
   - **Accessibility:** It is easier for patients in metropolitan regions to receive healthcare services, particularly if they have mobility impairments or reside in underprivileged areas.
   - **Efficiency:** Lowers hospital and clinic wait times and crowding.
   - **Cost-effective:** Reduces the expenses related to providing healthcare, for both patients and providers.

5. **Challenges:**
   - **Digital Divide:** Some patients do not have access to internet connectivity or the required technologies.
   - **Data Security:** It's critical to protect the privacy and security of patient data.

11.1.3. **Remote Health Monitoring:**

Digital devices are used in remote health monitoring to gather medical data from patients and send it to healthcare providers for review and monitoring. It consists of remote monitoring systems, wearable technology, and mobile health applications.

**Important Elements:**

a. **Mobile Health Applications:**
   - These are programs that monitor health indicators and give users notifications, reminders, and insights.
   - **Example:** People can track their food, exercise, and sleep habits with the use of apps like MyFitnessPal and Fitbit.

b. **Wearable Devices:**
   - Wearable devices are gadgets that track vital indications including blood pressure, heart rate, and activity level. Examples of these include smartwatches and fitness trackers.
   - **Example:** The Apple Watch's abnormal heartbeat alarms and ECG capabilities can notify users and medical professionals about possible health problems.

c. **Remote Monitoring Systems:**

- Tools for ongoing chronic condition monitoring, such as glucose monitors for diabetics.
- **Example:** Consider continuous glucose monitors (CGMs), such as the Dexcom G6, which transmit glucose readings to the patient's doctor and smartphone.

d. **Advantages:**
- **Proactive Health Management:** Timely action is made possible by the early identification of possible health issues through ongoing monitoring.
- **Decreased Hospitalizations**: By keeping an eye on chronic illnesses on a regular basis, complications can be avoided and hospital admissions can be minimized.
- **Customized Care:** Medical professionals can better meet the needs of each patient by using data from monitoring devices to customize treatment regimens.

e. **Challenges:**
- **Data Correctness:** It's crucial to guarantee the dependability and correctness of the data that devices collect.
- **Patient Compliance:** Patients must regularly use the devices and follow instructions for remote monitoring to be effective.

### 11.1.4. Integration into Urban Planning

By creating the necessary infrastructure and implementing legislative measures, urban planning can facilitate the integration of telemedicine and remote health monitoring.

### 11.1.5. Infrastructure Development:
- **Broadband connection:** For telemedicine and remote monitoring, it is essential to guarantee that there is ubiquitous, high-speed internet connection.
  - **Example:** To assist telehealth services in the US, the FCC's Connect2Health effort seeks to map and enhance internet access.
- **Smart Cities**: Improving urban healthcare delivery can be achieved by incorporating health data systems into smart city frameworks.

o   **Example:** Telemedicine is a component of Barcelona's smart city initiative's urban health plan, which uses data from several sources to enhance public health results.

**11.1.6. Policy Initiatives:**

- **Support from Regulations:** Lawmakers must create telemedicine-related regulations, such as those pertaining to reimbursement and telehealth providers' licensure.
    - o   **Example:** The US increased Medicare coverage for telehealth services in 2020, which greatly increased the uptake of telemedicine.
- **Public Health Campaigns** can enhance adoption by informing the public about the advantages and accessibility of telemedicine and remote monitoring.
    - o   **Example:** As part of its Smart Nation project, Singapore's Ministry of Health conducts campaigns to promote telehealth services.

In summary, modernizing healthcare delivery requires the use of telemedicine and remote health monitoring, particularly in urban areas. Cities may assure more effective use of resources, better public health management, and improve accessibility to healthcare by utilizing these technologies. Collaborative efforts between the IT, healthcare, and urban planning sectors will be necessary for the successful integration of these technologies into urban planning, in addition to supporting legislation and strong infrastructure development.

## 11.2. Health Data Analytics

Urban planning, public health, and healthcare delivery can all be improved with the help of health data analytics, a potent instrument that makes use of massive datasets. It includes gathering, analyzing, and processing data pertaining to health in order to derive actionable insights that can inform policy and decision-making. This chapter provides a thorough explanation of health data analytics, emphasizing its elements, uses, advantages, and drawbacks. Examples are included when appropriate.

**11.2.1. Elements of Health Data Analytics:**

**11.2.1.1.   Data Collection:**

- **Electronic Health Records (EHRs):** Digitally stored, comprehensive patient records.
- **Wearable Devices:** Electronic devices that monitor body temperature and activity level.
- **Patient Surveys and Health Registries**: Information gathered from these sources.
- **Public Health Data**: Details gathered from surveillance systems and public health databases.

### 11.2.1.2. **Data Processing**:

- **Data Cleaning:** Eliminating errors and discrepancies from the data is known as data cleaning.
- **Data Integration:** Integrating data for a coherent view by combining information from multiple sources.
- **Data Storage:** Safely keeping information in databases and data warehouses is known as data storage.

### 11.2.1.3. **Data Analysis:**

- **Descriptive Analytics:** Summarizing historical data to determine what has transpired is known as descriptive analytics.
- **Predictive Analytics** is the practice of forecasting future events using statistical models and machine learning.
- **Prescriptive Analytics:** Action recommendations made using predictive models are known as prescriptive analytics.

## 11.2.2. Health Data Analytics Applications

### 11.2.2.1. Clinical Decision Support:

- **Example:** IBM Watson Health utilizes sophisticated analytics to help doctors diagnose conditions and recommend courses of action based on a sizable body of patient data and medical literature.

### 11.2.2.2. Personalized Health Care:

- **Example:** As demonstrated by programs like the Precision Medicine Initiative in the United States, genomic data analysis enables the customization of medicines for specific individuals based on their genetic profiles.

### 11.2.2.3. Public Health Surveillance:

- **Example:** Health data analytics was utilized during the COVID-19 pandemic to monitor infection rates, simulate the virus's spread, and efficiently deploy resources. The COVID-19 dashboard from Johns Hopkins University gave the general public and decision-makers access to real-time data and analytics.

### 11.2.2.4. Planning and Resource Allocation:

- **Example:** Hospitals may better manage staffing levels, bed capacity, and supply chain logistics with the use of predictive analytics. Predictive models, for example, can foresee the surge of patients during flu season, enabling better planning.

### 11.2.2.5. Socioeconomic Determinants of Health and Health Equity:

- **Example:** To identify at-risk populations and create focused interventions to address health disparities, analytics systems such as Healthify gather and analyze data on Social Determinants of Health (SDOH).

### 11.2.3. Benefits of Health Data Analytics:

1. **Better Patient Results:** Health data analytics helps physicians make decisions that result in better patient care and results by giving them relevant information.
2. **Enhanced Efficiency:** By automating data processing, healthcare professionals can spend more time and energy on patient care rather than interpreting large amounts of data.
3. **Cost savings:** By detecting and managing diseases early on, predictive analytics can identify high-risk individuals and save expensive interventions.
4. **Informed Policy Making**: By utilizing health data analytics, urban planners and legislators can create more effective public health plans and initiatives.

### 11.2.4. Health Data Analytics' Challenges

### 11.2.4.1. Data Security and Privacy: It is crucial to protect the integrity and confidentiality of health data. Breach can do serious harm to people and erode public confidence.

### 11.2.4.2. Data Integration: It can be difficult to combine data from several sources (such as wearable technology, public health databases, and EHRs) because of variations in data formats, standards, and quality.

**11.2.4.3. Data Integrity:** Incomplete or inaccurate data might result in inaccurate conclusions and choices. Ensuring data quality is essential to obtaining trustworthy analytics.

**11.2.4.4. Interoperability:** The adoption of incompatible technology by various healthcare systems and devices makes it difficult to communicate and evaluate data easily.

**11.2.5.      Integration into Urban Planning**

In order to create healthier cities, urban planners can make use of health data analytics. This include figuring out the population's health requirements, forecasting health trends, and creating structures and regulations that support public health.

**11.2.5.1. Health Impact Assessment (HIAs):**
- Analyzing possible health effects of new urban development initiatives and regulations using data analytics.
- **Example:** The San Francisco Department of Public Health makes sure that decisions about urban design advance community health by using HIAs.

**11.2.5.2. Initiatives for Smart Cities:**
- Incorporating health data into smart city systems to track and enhance indicators related to urban health in real-time.
- **Example:** Barcelona's smart city projects use sensors and data analytics to track environmental parameters that affect public health, such as noise levels and air quality.

**11.2.5.3. Accessibility and Transportation:**
- Examining data on transportation and healthcare access to guarantee fair access to medical care.
- **Example:** The Vision Zero program in New York City employs data analytics to pinpoint and reduce traffic accident hotspots, enhancing safety for bicyclists and pedestrians.

In summary, an essential instrument at the nexus of IT and urban planning is health data analytics. It makes it possible to turn unprocessed health data into useful insights that can improve patient care, optimize healthcare operations, and guide urban development choices. In order to successfully apply health data analytics, issues with data privacy, integration, quality, and interoperability must be resolved. These initiatives aim to enhance urban living conditions and public health outcomes by utilizing data-driven approaches in cities, making them healthier, more efficient, and more egalitarian.

## 11.3. Personalized Healthcare Solutions

An important development in the nexus of IT, healthcare, and urban planning is personalized healthcare solutions. These approaches center on adjusting medical care to each patient's unique traits while accounting for lifestyle, environmental, and hereditary variables. Optimizing resource allocation, raising patient satisfaction, and improving results are all possible with personalized healthcare. This chapter provides a thorough analysis of customized healthcare solutions, emphasizing its elements, uses, advantages, and interaction with urban planning with concrete examples.

11.3.1. **Parts of a Personalized Healthcare Solutions:**

11.3.1.1. **Genomic Data:**

- **Genetic Testing:** Using DNA analysis to determine a person's genetic susceptibility to an illness.
- **Example:** Based on a person's genetic profile, companies such as 23andMe offer genetic testing services that provide insights into potential health risks.

11.3.1.2. **Electronic Health Records (EHRs):**

- **Comprehensive Information:** EHRs hold a great deal of patient information, such as medical history, current conditions, and results.
- **Example:** The EHR platform from Epic Systems combines genomic information with conventional medical records to enable individualized treatment regimens.

11.3.1.3. **Wearable Technology**:

- **Constant Monitoring:** Wearable technology, such as smartwatches, monitors sleep habits, physical activity, and vital signs.
- **Example:** The Apple Watch has health monitoring functions such as alerts for irregular heartbeat, blood oxygen levels, and electrocardiograms.

11.3.1.4. **Platforms for Health Analytics:**

- **Analytics and Data Integration:** Platforms that combine and examine data from various sources to produce insights that may be put to use are known as data integration and analysis platforms.

- **Example:** IBM Watson Health leverages AI to evaluate enormous datasets, assisting physicians in creating individualized treatment regimens based on patient-specific information and the most recent medical research.

**11.3.1.5. Applications for Mobile Health:**

- **Engaging Patients:** Applications that assist users in keeping track of their prescriptions, managing their health, and interacting with medical professionals.
- **Example:** Based on user input and activity data, MyFitnessPal and other health applications offer individualized recommendations.

**11.3.2.      Personalized Healthcare Solutions' Applications:**

**11.3.2.1. Personalized Medicine:**

- **Customized Care:** Formulating remedies according to each patient's unique genetic composition.
- For instance, pharmacogenomics can be used to ascertain a patient's optimal medicine and dosage depending on their genetic composition. For example, certain cancer therapies are designed to specifically target certain genetic abnormalities.

**11.3.2.2.  Handling Chronic Illnesses:**

- **Continuous Monitoring:** Keeping an eye on and managing chronic conditions with wearable technology and smartphone apps.
- As an illustration, diabetics can precisely adjust their insulin dosage by using Continuous Glucose Monitors (CGMs), such as the Dexcom G6, which provide real-time glucose readings and trends.

**11.3.2.3.  Preventive Healthcare:**

- **Risk Assessment** is the process of determining who is most likely to develop a particular ailment and putting preventative measures in place.
- For instance, genetic testing for BRCA1 and BRCA2 mutations can assist women in identifying their risk factors for ovarian and breast cancers and in implementing preventative measures like routine surgery or heightened surveillance.

**11.3.2.4.  Behavioural Health:**

- **Mental Health Monitoring:** Using applications to monitor stress levels, mood, and other mental health indicators is known as mental health monitoring.

- For instance, the Headspace app uses user input and behavioral patterns to provide tailored meditation and mental health tools.

### 11.3.3. Advantages of Tailored Healthcare Solutions:

### 11.3.3.1. Enhanced Patient Results

- **Effectiveness:** Individualized treatments are frequently more successful.
- **Decreased Side Effects:** The likelihood of unfavorable reactions is decreased with customized drugs.

### 11.3.3.2. Patient Involvement and Contentment:

- **Empowerment:** When therapies are customized to the individual, patients are more involved in their care.
- **Convenience:** Wearable technology and mobile apps let patients better control their health.

### 11.3.3.3. Cost Efficiency:

- **Preventive Care:** By implementing tailored preventive measures and early detection, the need for expensive treatments can be decreased.
- **Resource Optimisation:** Better resource allocation based on specific patient needs is known as resource optimization.

### 11.3.4. Integration into Urban Planning

When policies and infrastructure are in place, urban planning may greatly facilitate and improve the implementation of individualized healthcare solutions.

### 11.3.4.1. Accessibility of Healthcare:

- **Distribution of Services:** Ensuring that all urban dwellers have access to healthcare facilities that provide individualized treatments.
- One example would be the integration of telemedicine centers to enable access to individualized healthcare services in underprivileged neighborhoods.

### 11.3.4.2. Infrastructure of Smart Cities:

- **Data Connectivity** refers to providing a stable data infrastructure and fast internet access to enable telemedicine and health data analytics.
- As an illustration, Barcelona's smart city projects involve the use of IoT devices and sensors to gather health data and enhance public health services.

### 11.3.4.3. Policies for Public Health:

- **Standards and Regulations:** Creating guidelines to facilitate the incorporation of individualized healthcare into the public health system.
- **Example:** The General Data Protection Regulation (GDPR) of the European Union has rules that encourage the safe management of health data, making it easier to apply tailored health solutions.

### 11.3.4.4. Initiatives for Community Health:

- **Engagement and Education:** Initiatives to inform the general people about the advantages of individualized medicine and the means of obtaining it.
- As an illustration, public health initiatives that encourage the use of wearable technology and health applications are part of Singapore's Smart Nation strategy.

### 11.3.5. Challenges and Considerations:

### 11.3.5.1. Security and Privacy of Data:

- **Protection of Personal Health Information:** Making sure that private health information is secure and kept private.
- **Compliance:** Following laws such as GDPR in the EU and HIPAA in the US.

### 11.3.5.2. Interoperability:

- **Standardization** is the process of creating and approving guidelines for the interchange of data between various medical equipment and systems.

### 11.3.5.3. Accessibility and Cost:

- **Equity:** Ensuring that all societal groups may afford and obtain tailored healthcare treatments.

### 11.3.5.4. Moral Aspects to Consider:

- **Informed Consent:** Ensuring that patients are aware of and agree to the use of their data for individualized medical care is known as informed consent.

In summary, the convergence of IT and urban planning has resulted in a major breakthrough in the provision of medical care: personalized healthcare solutions. These solutions provide customized treatments that have the potential to improve patient outcomes, increase efficiency, and lower costs by utilizing genetic data, wearable technology, and health analytics. To ensure equal access and efficient utilization, the successful implementation of personalized healthcare in urban contexts necessitates strong infrastructure, regulations that support it, and public engagement. Cities may improve the well-being of their citizens by utilizing the power of personalized healthcare through strategic planning and cross-sector collaboration.

# Chapter 12: Education and Digital Literacy in Smart Cities

## 12.1. Smart Classrooms and E-Learning

Through the use of cutting-edge technologies, smart classrooms and e-learning are transforming education and enabling individualized, dynamic, and interesting learning experiences. Fostering educational innovation and accessibility requires an awareness of how these technologies are integrated in urban surroundings, which is critical for an IT and urban planning specialist. This is a thorough explanation of smart classrooms and e-learning, with examples when feasible, emphasizing the elements, uses, advantages, and drawbacks of each.

12.1.1. **Smart Classrooms:** Utilizing digital tools and technologies, smart classrooms improve instruction and learning. The goal of these classrooms is to give teachers and students a more engaged and cooperative learning environment.

1. **Important Components:**
   a. **Interactive Whiteboards:**
      - Teachers can engage students, annotate materials, and conduct interactive classes using digital whiteboards.
      - **Example:** SMART Boards are frequently utilized in classrooms to support engaging instruction.
   b. **Digital Learning Platforms:**
      - Software programs that give teachers and students access to resources, homework, and communication capabilities.
      - **Example:** Google Classroom enables paperless assignment creation, distribution, and grading for teachers.
   c. **Virtual Reality (VR) and Augmented Reality (AR):**
      - Technologies that produce engaging educational opportunities.
      - **Example:** ClassVR offers virtual reality headsets and instructional materials in science and history, enabling students to investigate ancient cultures or the human body in three dimensions.
   d. **Response Systems for Students:**

- Tools that facilitate in-class communication and real-time feedback.
- **Example:** Clickers or applications such as Kahoot! let students respond to questions and take part in surveys in class.

e. **Learning Management Systems (LMS):**
- Platforms that oversee the management of instructional course administration, documentation, tracking, and delivery.
- **Example:** Many academic institutions use the open-source LMS Moodle to administer and deliver online courses.

2. **Applications:**

a. **Flipped Classrooms:**
- While in class, students engage in hands-on activities and conversations, they also view videos and complete interactive modules to learn new subject online.
- **Example:** Khan Academy offers video lessons that students can view at home, freeing up teachers to concentrate on problem-solving exercises in the classroom.

b. **Collaborative Education:**
- Using digital technologies, smart classrooms promote group projects and teamwork.
- **Example:** Microsoft Teams for Education enables real-time resource sharing and project collaboration among students.

c. **Special Education:**
- For pupils with specific needs, tailored learning strategies are supported by smart technologies.
- **Example:** Adaptive learning systems and speech-to-text software facilitate students with impairments' efficient access to instructional materials.

12.1.2. **E-Learning:** The use of electronic technology to access educational materials outside of a traditional classroom is known as e-learning. It includes a broad spectrum of educational options, ranging from wholly online programs to hybrid models that blend online and in-person training.

1. **Important Elements:**

a. **Web-Based Classes and MOOCs:**

- Massive Open Online Courses (MOOCs): Numerous online courses from different universities cover a broad range of subjects.
- **Example:** Anyone with an internet connection can access classes from Stanford, MIT, Harvard, and other colleges through Coursera and edX.

b. **Virtual Classrooms and Webinars:**
- Interactive online courses and seminars delivered via the internet.
- **Example:** Zoom and Webex are well-liked tools for holding webinars and live online classes.

c. **Mobile Learning:**
- Mobile device accessibility to educational content enables learning while on the go.
- **Example:** Duolingo allows users to learn languages at any time and from any location by providing an entertaining smartphone app.

d. **Resources and Digital Libraries:**
- Books, research articles, and instructional resources stored online.
- **Example:** Academics and students can access thousands of scholarly books and articles through JSTOR.

## 2. Applications:

a. **Self-Directed Learning:**
- Pupils are free to study at their own speed and go over content again as needed to fully understand it.
- **Example:** LinkedIn Learning provides courses on skill development and career advancement that students can finish at their own speed.

b. **Blended Learning:**
- Blends traditional teaching techniques with digital media found online.
- **Example:** A high school might hold regular in-person sessions for discussions and laboratories in addition to using an LMS to deliver online coursework.

c. **Corporate Training:**
- Employers use e-learning platforms to give their staff members continual training and opportunities for professional growth.
- **Example:** A variety of courses are available on platforms such as Udemy for Business to improve the skills and knowledge of employees.

## 3. Advantages

a. **Accessibility:**

- E-learning and smart classrooms open up access to education for more people, especially those living in impoverished or distant places.
- **Example:** e-learning platforms can be used by rural schools to give students access to high-quality learning materials that might not be available in their area.

## b. Adaptability:

- Different learning styles and demands can be accommodated by allowing students to learn at their own pace and on their own time.
- **Example:** To upskill without interfering with their job schedules, working professionals might enroll in online courses.

## c. Engagement:

- Rich, interactive multimedia content improves learning and keeps students interested.
- **Example:** Interactive simulations in scientific classes might help students comprehend and remember difficult ideas.

## d. Economical:

- Minimizes the need for materials and physical infrastructure, which could save schooling costs.
- **Example:** The necessity for costly physical textbooks is eliminated by the use of digital textbooks and internet resources.

## 12.1.3. Challenges:

### 12.1.3.1. Digital Divide:

- Not every student has the same level of access to the required technology and internet availability.
- **Example:** Due to a lack of gadgets or dependable internet, students in low-income households may find it difficult to engage in online learning.

### 12.1.3.2. Training of Teachers:

- To employ new technology and incorporate them into their teaching techniques, teachers must receive training.
- **Example:** In order to assist teachers in making the switch to smart classrooms and online learning environments, professional development programs are crucial.

### 12.1.3.3. Quality Control:

- Ensuring the reliability and caliber of online education and resources.
- **Example:** Standardized tests and accreditation can support the upkeep of good standards in online education.

### 12.1.3.4. Privacy and Security:

- Maintaining a secure online learning environment and safeguarding student data.
- **Example:** It's critical to have strong cybersecurity safeguards in place and teach pupils about safe online behavior.

### 12.1.4. Integration into Urban Planning:

Through legislative initiatives and infrastructure development, urban planning may play a crucial role in facilitating the introduction of smart classrooms and e-learning.

### 12.1.4.1. Infrastructure Development:

- Guaranteeing everyone access to high-speed internet and offering free Wi-Fi in public areas.
- **Example:** Municipal broadband programs in places like Chattanooga, Tennessee, give all citizens access to high-speed internet, facilitating e-learning.

### 12.1.4.2. Policy Initiatives:

- Creating regulations that support the use of technology in the classroom and deal with issues of digital equity.
- **Example:** To enable all students to engage in remote learning, the Department of Education in New York City, for instance, has put in place initiatives to give students gadgets and internet connection.

### 12.1.4.3. Hubs for Community Learning:

- Establishing community centers with teachers on staff and digital resource availability to facilitate e-learning.
- **Example:** The Learning Hubs program in San Francisco offers secure areas with internet connectivity and instructional assistance to enable students to engage in virtual learning.

In summary, education is changing because of smart classrooms and e-learning, which make learning more flexible, interesting, and accessible. For students of all ages, these technologies have the potential to greatly improve both the learning process and the results. However, issues with digital equity, teacher preparation, quality assurance, and security must be resolved for the implementation to be successful. Policymakers and urban planners are essential in building the rules and infrastructure required to guarantee that the advantages of these breakthroughs are available to all. Through the incorporation of e-learning and smart classrooms into urban planning, cities may promote an inclusive and progressive learning environment.

## 12.2. Bridging the Digital Divide

In order to guarantee fair access to information and communication technology (ICT), which in turn permits more extensive socioeconomic development, it is imperative that the digital divide be bridged. Addressing the digital divide requires a multifaceted strategy that encompasses infrastructure development, legislative measures, community participation, and technology adoption, as an IT and Urban Planning Specialist can attest to. This article provides a thorough analysis of methods for bridging the digital divide with real-world examples.

12.2.1. **Recognizing the Digital Divide:**

The difference between people and communities who have access to contemporary information and communication technology and those who do not is known as the "*digital divide*." Access to the internet, the availability of digital equipment, digital literacy, and the capacity to use and profit from ICT are just a few ways in which this disparity may show up.

12.2.2.　　**Aspects of Digital Divide**

12.2.2.1. **Infrastructure Access:**

- **Broadband Availability:** Making sure all areas, especially rural and underserved metropolitan areas, have access to high-speed internet.
- **Example:** The lack of broadband infrastructure in rural areas of the United States frequently results in poor or nonexistent internet connection.

12.2.2.2. **Cost-Effectiveness:**

- **Cost of Devices and Services:** The capacity to pay for internet services and buy gadgets like laptops and cellphones.
- **Example:** Many urban low-income communities' people are unable to purchase modern digital equipment or high-speed internet connections.

12.2.2.3. **Digital Literacy:**

- **Skills and Education:** The capacity to communicate, learn, and work with digital technologies in an efficient manner.
- **Example:** People in marginalized communities and older persons might not know how to use digital tools well.

12.2.2.4. **Significance and Application:**

- **Meaningful Use:** Providing people with digital services and content that are applicable to their requirements and easily incorporated into their everyday life.
- **Example:** One example would be offering services and information that are tailored to the language and culture of certain populations.

12.2.3. **Techniques for Closing the Digital Divide:**

12.2.3.1. **Development of Infrastructure**

a. **Increasing Access to Broadband:**

- Invest in infrastructure to give underserved urban and rural communities access to high-speed internet.
- **Example:** The Rural Digital Opportunity Fund established by the FCC seeks to increase broadband availability to millions of underserved rural American homes and businesses.

b. **Public Wi-Fi Projects:**

- Provide free public Wi-Fi at parks, community centers, libraries, and other areas.
- **Example:** The LinkNYC program in New York City offers free high-speed Wi-Fi through kiosks positioned all across the city.

12.2.3.2. **Affordability Initiatives:**

a. **Internet Services with Subsidies:**

- Provide low-income homes with internet services at a discount.
- **Example:** Eligible low-income families can get affordable internet through Comcast's Internet Essentials program.

**b. Programs for Device Access:**

- Give students and low-income people digital gadgets for free or at a reduced cost.
- **Example:** Children in impoverished nations receive inexpensive laptops from the One Laptop Per Child (OLPC) program.

## 12.2.3.3. Training in Digital Literacy and Skills:

**a. Programs for Community Training:**

- Create training programs that impart digital skills to a range of populations, such as minorities, retirees, and low-income families.
- **Example:** Google's Grow with Google program provides free resources, tools, and training to support people in developing their businesses, careers, and skill sets.

**b. School-Based programs:**

- Include instruction on digital literacy in school curricula and give educators training.
- **Example:** The UK's Computing at School (CAS) initiative provides teachers with the tools and instruction they need to teach computers.

## 12.2.3.4. Advocacy and Policy:

**a. Supportive Legislation:**

- Promote legislation that encourages digital inclusion, such as financing for increased internet availability and initiatives to improve digital literacy.
- **Example:** In order to more effectively target expansion efforts, the US Broadband DATA Act requires the collecting of precise broadband availability data.

**b. Plans for Digital Equity:**

- Create thorough plans that include every facet of digital inclusion on a local, state, and federal level.
- **Example:** The City of Seattle's Digital Equity Initiative provides guidelines for improving everyone's access to, proficiency in, and opportunities in the digital world.

## 12.2.3.5. Public-Private Collaborations:

**a. Combined Efforts:**

- Involve government organizations, non-profits, and the commercial sector in addressing the digital gap together.
- **Example:** To give public housing residents access to the internet, the U.S. Department of Housing and Urban Development (HUD) is working with a number of commercial and public sector partners on the ConnectHomeUSA initiative.

## 12.2.4.  Instances of Successful Projects

### 12.2.4.1. Barcelona, Spain:

- **Smart City Initiatives:** Increasing public Wi-Fi coverage, encouraging digital literacy, and guaranteeing equitable access to digital services are just a few of the measures Barcelona has put into place.
- **Example:** The city's WiFiBCN project helps close the digital gap by providing free internet connection in a variety of public areas.

### 12.2.4.2. Kenya

- **Mobile Connectivity:** Kenya has increased digital access by utilizing mobile technology. Adoption of mobile internet has also been fueled by the extensive use of mobile money services like M-Pesa.
- **Example:** Consider the Mawingu initiative, a collaboration between Microsoft and regional ISPs that exploits TV white spaces to offer reasonably priced internet in rural areas.

### 12.2.4.3. India

- **Digital India Initiative:** The goal of the government-led Digital India Initiative is to make India a knowledge economy and society that is enabled by technology.
- **Example:** The BharatNet initiative intends to provide high-speed internet to each of India's 250,000 gram panchayats, or local councils.

## 12.2.5.  Obstacles in Crossing the Digital Divide:

### 12.2.5.1. Finance and Investing

- It can be difficult to secure the funding required to construct and maintain digital infrastructure, particularly in rural and low-income areas.

### 12.2.5.2. Coordination and Implementation:

- While necessary, effective coordination between various stakeholders—including governmental organizations, commercial enterprises, and nonprofit organizations—is frequently challenging.

### 12.2.5.3. Sustainability:

- Making sure that programs for digital inclusion are long-lasting and flexible enough to adjust to changing requirements and technologies.

### 12.2.5.4. Language and Cultural Barriers:

- Language and cultural barriers must be taken into consideration when creating services and content that are relevant to a wide range of users.

In summary, in the digital age, promoting social and economic inclusion requires closing the digital divide. Implementing comprehensive solutions that involve infrastructure development, affordable initiatives, digital literacy training, supportive legislation, and public-private partnerships is essential for an IT and urban planning specialist. By tackling these issues and taking inspiration from globally effective efforts, we can build a more connected and inclusive society where everyone can reap the rewards of technological progress.

## 12.3. Promoting Lifelong Learning

Encouraging lifelong learning is crucial for adjusting to the quick changes in social, technological, and economic aspects of modern society. Lifelong learning is the ongoing, self-driven pursuit of information for one's own or one's career's advancement. You can contribute to the design and implementation of infrastructures and systems that support lifelong learning as an IT and urban planning specialist. This entails developing settings that facilitate inclusive, adaptable, and accessible education. This is a thorough explanation of encouraging lifelong learning with examples.

### 12.3.1. Crucial Components of Lifelong Learning:

### 12.3.1.1. Accessibility:

- Guaranteeing that educational opportunities are accessible to all individuals, irrespective of their location, socioeconomic condition, age, or history.
- **Example:** Giving resources and courses that are accessible online from any location with an internet connection is one example.

12.3.1.2. **Adaptability**:

- Supplying educational options that work with a range of schedules and circumstances.
- **Example:** Self-paced online courses, for instance, let students study whenever it's most convenient for them.

12.3.1.3. **Inclusivity:**

- Addressing the requirements of a diverse student body, which includes people with disabilities, people with varying learning styles, and people from different cultural backgrounds.
- **Example:** Creating courses that are available in text, audio, and video forms and include accommodations like screen readers or subtitles.

12.3.1.4. **Community Participation:**

- Promoting community involvement and assistance with educational projects.
- **Example:** To promote a learning community, local libraries sponsor study groups and workshops.

12.3.1.5. **Integration of Technology:**

- Use technology to increase accessibility and improve educational opportunities.
- **Example:** Using virtual reality, smartphone apps, and AI-powered tailored learning systems are a few examples.

12.3.2. **Strategies to Encourage Lifelong Learning**

12.3.2.1. **Creating Online Learning Environments:**

- Establishing online learning environments with a range of materials, courses, and teaching aids.
- **Example:** Students all over the world can access a variety of courses from prestigious universities and institutes through Coursera, Udemy, and edX.

12.3.2.2. **Creating Centers for Community Learning:**

- Establishing physical locations with internet connectivity, educational materials, and staff members who have received training to assist students.
- **Example:** The Fab Lab network provides training courses and cutting-edge manufacturing tools to the general public in order to encourage experiential learning and creativity.

12.3.2.3. **Putting Workplace Learning Programs in Place:**
- Encouraging companies to give their staff members continual opportunity for training and development.
- **Example:** Google's "20% Time" strategy encourages employees to dedicate 20% of their work to projects that pique their interest, so promoting ongoing education and creativity.

12.3.2.4. **Developing Legislative Directives and Incentives:**
- Governments can encourage lifelong learning by enacting laws and providing financial aid for public education programs, among other measures.
- **Example:** The Erasmus+ initiative of the European Union supports lifelong learning and mobility by providing funding for educational and training opportunities throughout Europe.

12.3.2.5. **Open Educational Resources (OER) Promotion:**
- Encouraging the creation and application of freely accessible educational resources that anybody may use, adapt, and share.
- **Example:** MIT OpenCourseWare encourages self-directed learning by offering free access to course materials from a variety of MIT courses.

12.3.3. **Examples and Case Studies**

12.3.3.1. **Spain's Barcelona Activa:**
- **Overview:** Barcelona Activa is a career advisory service, training program, and workshop provider that promotes lifelong learning.
- **Initiatives:** To promote ongoing professional development, it provides a range of online and in-person courses in technology, entrepreneurship, and professional skills.

12.3.3.2. **FutureLearn, United Kingdom:**
- **Overview:** FutureLearn is an online learning platform that provides top universities with courses, programs, and degrees.
- **Impact:** It promotes lifelong learning globally by offering accessible and adaptable learning opportunities across a broad range of subjects.

12.3.3.3. **SkillsFuture Singapore:**
- **Overview:** Regardless of one's starting point, SkillsFuture is a national initiative in Singapore that aims to provide everyone the chance to reach their greatest potential throughout life.

- **Programs:** It consists of programs like SkillsFuture Credit, which gives residents credits to use toward authorized courses relevant to skills, and SkillsFuture Work-Study Programs, which combine education with real-world work experience.

12.3.3.4. **The Khan Academy:**

- **Overview:** Khan Academy is a non-profit that provides free online instruction, practice, and courses in a range of areas.
- **Impact:** Students of all ages can benefit from individualized learning experiences that allow them to learn at their own speed and on their own schedule.

12.3.3.5. **Telecentre.Org Foundation:**

- **Overview:** An international network of community-based facilities that offer technology and educational materials.
- **Initiatives:** To support digital inclusion and lifelong learning, these centers provide underprivileged populations with ICT training, educational programs, and online learning possibilities.

## 12.3.4. Role of Urban Planning in Lifelong Learning

The creation of surroundings that support lifelong learning is greatly influenced by urban planning. This covers the creation of physical environments, infrastructure, and policy to facilitate lifelong learning and education.

### 12.3.4.1. Making Spaces That Are Learning-Friendly:

- Converting multipurpose areas like community centers, public parks, and libraries into venues that can be used for education.
- **Example:** The Idea Store in London offers a contemporary and hospitable setting for lifelong learning by fusing classroom areas, community activities, and library resources.

### 12.3.4.2. Making Certain Digital Infrastructure:

- Constructing a solid digital infrastructure to enable online learning platforms and offer high-speed internet access.
- **Example:** Municipal broadband programs in places like Chattanooga, Tennessee, give all citizens access to high-speed internet, promoting digital literacy and online education.

### 12.3.4.3. Policy Formulation:

- Putting into practice laws that support lifelong learning and allocate funds for educational projects.

- **Example:** The City of Helsinki's Education Policy describes methods for encouraging lifelong learning via digital learning projects, adult education courses, and job training programs.

### 12.3.4.4. Public-Private Partnerships (PPP):

- Promoting cooperation in order to create learning opportunities between companies, government, and educational institutions.
- **Example:** The IBM-sponsored P-TECH (Pathways in Technology Early College High School) model blends career training, college, and high school to provide students with avenues for success in both their academic and professional endeavors.

In summary, encouraging lifelong learning is crucial for social inclusion, economic progress, and personal development. You can have a significant impact on the development and implementation of systems that facilitate ongoing learning as an IT and urban planning specialist. To help close the achievement gap in education and guarantee that everyone has the opportunity to learn and develop throughout their lives, you can build digital platforms, community learning centers, workplace learning programs, supportive policies, and public-private partnerships.

# Chapter 13: Governance and Citizen Engagement

## 13.1. E-Government Services

The term "*E-Government Services*" refers to the use of digital technologies by government agencies to provide information, services, and interactions with businesses, citizens, and other arms of government. The goal of these services is to make government operations more transparent, efficient, and accessible. It is vital to comprehend the implementation and effects of e-government services in order to improve urban governance and citizens' quality of life. The following is a detailed explanation of e-government services, backed by examples:

13.1.1. **E-Government Service Components**

13.1.1.1.  **Online Service Delivery:**

- Online access to government services, including tax filing, license renewals, and permit applications.
- **Example:** the US Internal Revenue Service (IRS) enables individuals to electronically file their taxes using its e-file system.

13.1.1.2.  **Platforms for Digital Communication:**

- Channels for direct public-government communication, such as social media, email, and official government applications.
- **Example:** the GOV.UK Notify service is used by the UK government to notify residents via text and email regarding applications or public services.

13.1.1.3.  **Open Data Projects:**

- Government datasets are made accessible to the public to encourage innovation, openness, and well-informed decision-making.
- **Example:** the open data portal for the US government, Data.gov, gives users access to datasets from numerous governmental agencies.:

13.1.1.4.  **E-Participation (Online Engagement):**

- Online consultations, electronic voting, and participatory budgeting are a few examples of platforms and tools that encourage public participation in decision-making.
- **Example:** The Better Reykjavik site in Iceland enables users to submit and vote on suggestions for enhancing the city.

## 13.1.1.5. **Integrated Government Services:**

- Systems that combine different government departments to offer citizens smooth services.
- **Example:** The X-Road platform in Estonia links various government databases to enable streamlined and integrated e-services.

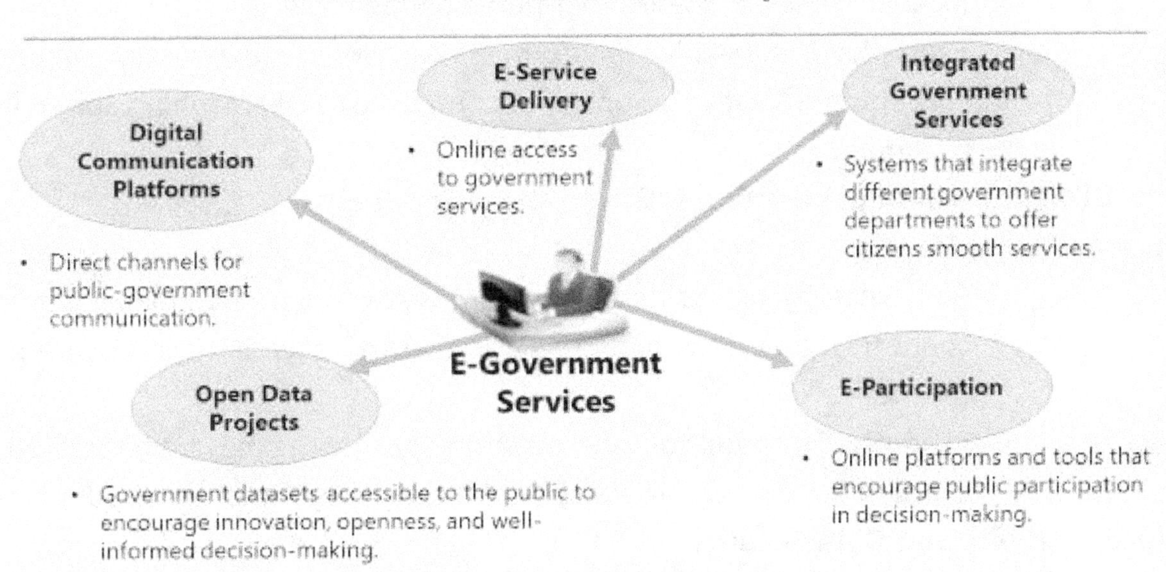



**Source:** Smart Cities: *The Technology Transforming Urban Living*, GoodMan Series, (Patrick Mukosha, 2024).

*Figure 8: e-Government Service Components*

## 13.1.2. **Advantages of E-Government Services:**

### 13.1.2.1. **Enhanced Convenience and Accessibility**

- Services are available to citizens from anywhere at any time.
- **Example:** SingPass from the Singaporean government offers a single digital identity for over 340 online government services.

### 13.1.2.2. **Increased Effectiveness and Financial Savings:**

- Minimizes the need for paper documents and in-person meetings, simplifying government processes and cutting expenses.
- **Example:** postal expenses have been greatly decreased by the Danish government's e-Boks service, which enables safe digital contact between citizens and the public sector.

### 13.1.2.3. **More Accountability and Transparency:**

- Digital communication channels and open data encourage transparency and provide people the power to hold their government responsible.
- **Example:** Brazil's Transparency Portal promotes accountability and openness by offering comprehensive data on government spending and the budget.

13.1.2.4. **Enhanced Involvement of Citizens:**

- Citizens can participate more actively in governance and decision-making processes thanks to e-participation tools.
- **Example:** The Decidim platform in Barcelona allows users to submit concepts and cast votes online to contribute to city planning and policy-making.

13.1.3. **Difficulties in Implementing E-Government Services**

13.1.3.1. **Digital Divide:**

- Guaranteeing all residents, even those without dependable internet connectivity or low digital literacy, equal access to e-government services.
- **Example:** The adoption of e-government services may be hampered by a lack of technology access in rural areas or among older populations.

13.1.3.2. **Privacy and Data Security:**

- Preserving citizens' privacy and shielding important data from online threats.
- **Example:** the 2015 hack on the U.S. Office of Personnel Management revealed millions of federal employees' personal information, underscoring the importance of strong cybersecurity defenses.

13.1.3.3. **Integration & Interoperability:**

- Ensuring the smooth integration of various government platforms and systems.
- **Example:** It can be difficult and expensive to integrate historical systems with new digital platforms, and it requires a high level of technical know-how.

13.1.3.4. **Adoption and Change Management:**

- Encouraging the adoption and efficient use of new digital tools by residents and government staff.

- **Example:** The effective execution of e-government projects might be hampered by citizens' low digital literacy or government employees' resistance to change.

### 13.1.4. Methods for Effectively Implementing E-Government

### 13.1.4.1. Developing Robust Digital Infrastructure:

- To support e-government services, investments should be made in dependable IT systems, secure servers, and fast internet.
- **Example:** the extensive internet infrastructure in South Korea has made it possible for e-government services to be widely adopted.

### 13.1.4.2. Safeguarding Data Privacy and Cybersecurity:

- Putting in place strict data protection laws and cybersecurity safeguards.
- **Example:** The General Data Protection Regulation (GDPR) of the European Union establishes stringent guidelines for data security and privacy that are applicable to e-government services.

### 13.1.4.3. Encouraging Digital Literacy:

- Supplying information and training to assist citizens and government workers in acquiring the required digital skills.
- **Example:** Estonia's e-Governance Academy offers materials and training to raise the level of digital literacy among its populace and public servants.

### 13.1.4.4. Encouraging Public-Private Collaborations:

- Working together with businesses in the private sector to take advantage of their resources and experience.
- **Example:** the development of India's Aadhaar project, a distinctive biometric identity system, which was made possible by private technology companies.

### 13.1.4.5. Creating Services Focused on Users:

- e-government services are created with the user in mind, making sure they are user-friendly and fulfill the needs of the public.
- **Example:** To produce user-friendly and easily available online services, the Government Digital Service (GDS) of the United Kingdom use a user-centered design methodology.

### 13.1.5. E-Government Initiative Success Stories

### 13.1.5.1. Estonia:

- **Overview:** Offering a wide range of digital services like e-residency, online voting, and digital signatures, Estonia is a global leader in e-government.
- **Impact:** Almost all government services, including tax filing and election voting, are now available online for Estonians, greatly increasing efficiency and ease.

### 13.1.5.2. **Singapore:**

- **Overview:** Using technology to enhance public services and quality of life is the goal of Singapore's Smart Nation effort.
- **Services:** Moments of Life app (integrating several services for different stages of life), SingPass, and MyInfo (a digital repository of personal data).
- **Impact:** Increased efficiency in the public sector and high rates of digital service adoption.

### 13.1.5.3. **Rwanda:**

- **Overview:** For online access to government services, use the Irembo platform as a one-stop shop.
- **Services:** Contains services like land registration, driving license renewals, and birth certificate applications.
- **Impact:** Lessened administrative hassles and better access to government services, particularly in rural areas.

### 13.1.5.4. **United Arab Emirates:**

- **Overview:** The provision of smooth and effective services via the DubaiNow app and other platforms is the main goal of the UAE's e-Government policy.
- **Services:** Bill payment, visa applications, and doctor appointments are examples of services.
- **Impact:** Notable advancements in the provision of government services and high consumer satisfaction.

### 13.1.6. **Role of Urban Planning in E-Government Services**

Urban planning ensures that the policies and infrastructure needed to facilitate digital transformation are in place, which is critical to the effective deployment of e-government services.

### 13.1.6.1. **Development of Infrastructure:**

- Preparing both urban and rural regions for digital infrastructure and high-speed internet connectivity.
- **Example:** Include broadband infrastructure in plans for urban development to guarantee widespread connectivity.

13.1.6.2. **Initiatives for Smart Cities:**
- Utilizing e-government services to enhance urban living as a component of larger smart city initiatives.
- **Example:** integrated digital services for energy management, public transit, and citizen interaction are part of Barcelona's smart city initiatives.

13.1.6.3. **Regulation and Policy:**
- Creating policies, such as data privacy laws and digital inclusion programs, to encourage the adoption and use of e-government services.
- **Example:** The Digital Playbook of New York City describes tactics for community involvement, data openness, and digital service delivery.

13.1.6.4. **Access Points and Public Areas:**
- Establishing public access sites where people can use e-government services, such libraries and community centers.
- **Example:** free internet access and digital literacy courses are provided by public libraries to assist the public in using e-government services.

In summary, the way citizens engage with the government might be completely changed by e-government services, which would increase service accessibility, effectiveness, and transparency. Promoting and executing these services as an IT and Urban Planning Specialist entails tackling issues with digital infrastructure, cybersecurity, digital literacy, and change management. You may contribute to the development of a more effective and inclusive digital government that satisfies the demands of all citizens by utilizing proven tactics and taking inspiration from worldwide examples.

## 13.2. Participatory Platforms for Citizens

Digital tools and systems known as participatory platforms are made with the intention of directly involving citizens in governance, urban planning, and decision-making processes. These platforms improve public participation in democracy by giving people a way to express their ideas, make proposals, and work with the government. You are essential to the development and implementation of these platforms as an IT and urban planning specialist, helping to make sure they are safe, efficient, and inclusive. This is a thorough explanation of citizen participation platforms with examples.

### 13.2.1. **Important Characteristics of Interactive Platforms:**

### 13.2.1.1. **User-Friendly Interfaces**

- Create user-friendly interfaces that are accessible to people of various ages and technological ability.
- **Example:** The Better Reykjavik platform provides a simple user interface via which residents can quickly submit and vote on city-related ideas.

### 13.2.1.2. **Accessibility and Inclusivity:**

- Make sure the platforms are multilingual and accessible to individuals with disabilities in order to serve a variety of demographics.
- **Example:** The Decidim platform in Barcelona offers elements that make participation inclusive, like support for multiple languages and characteristics that make it accessible to people with impairments.

### 13.2.1.3. **Transparency and Responsibility:**

- Put in place tools that make it possible to monitor decisions and proposals, giving information on how public input is used transparently.
- **Example:** The Participatory Budgeting platform in Paris ensures transparency by publishing comprehensive data on the budget's allocation process, which is dependent on public votes.

### 13.2.1.4. **Privacy and Security:**

- Make sure that privacy policies are transparent and easy to understand, and safeguard user data with strong security methods.
- **Example:** Estonia's e-governance system uses blockchain technology to protect citizen data and guarantee the accuracy of democratic procedures.

### 13.2.1.5. **Integrating with Current Systems:**

- Make sure that participatory platforms can easily share data and synchronize processes with other government systems by integrating with them.
- **Example:** By integrating different e-government services, the GOV.UK platform enables a consistent approach to citizen participation and service delivery.

### 13.2.2. **Examples of Interactive Platforms**

### 13.2.2.1. Better Reykjavik (Iceland):

- **Overview:** An online forum where people can post suggestions for city improvements and cast their votes for them.
- **Impact:** The platform has been used by more than 60% of the city's citizens, which has resulted in the implementation of multiple citizen-initiated projects.

### 13.2.2.2. Decidim (Spain, Barcelona):

- **Overview:** An open-source platform for participatory democracy that enables people to plan, budget, and make policies.
- **Impact:** Promotes more involved citizens through a range of participatory mechanisms, such as policy consultations and local budgeting.

### 13.2.2.3. Budgeting by Participation (Paris, France):

- **Overview:** Projects to be funded by a portion of the city budget are proposed by citizens and put to a vote.
- **Impact:** Since its inception, millions of euros have been allotted to citizen-chosen projects, increasing public participation in financial decision-making.

### 13.2.2.4. Your Priorities (Estonia):

- **Overview:** A platform where people can vote on and provide ideas that the government can then take into consideration for execution.
- **Impact:** Enabled a number of regional and national projects, enhancing Estonia's standing as a pioneer in digital democracy.

### 13.2.2.5. Change.org:

- **Overview:** People can create and sign petitions on a variety of problems using this global platform.
- **Impact:** Numerous petitions have changed laws and procedures all throughout the world, proving the effectiveness of mass citizen activism.

### 13.2.3. Advantages of Participatory Platforms:

### 13.2.3.1. Increased Civic Engagement:

- Promotes increased involvement in politics, which results in citizens who are better informed and involved.
- **Example:** Decidim and similar platforms have raised public participation in local government decision-making.

### 13.2.3.2. Enhanced Confidence in the Government:

- Government and citizen trust is increased when decision-making procedures are open, accountable, and transparent.
- **Example:** Paris' Participatory Budgeting has enhanced the public's view of the government's dedication to citizen involvement.

### 13.2.3.3. Improved Decision-Making

- Policies and projects become more inclusive and comprehensive when different points of view are taken into account.
- **Example:** Reykjavik's platform has led to the execution of initiatives that truly represent the aspirations and requirements of the city's citizens.

### 13.2.3.4. Creativity & Innovation:

- Government officials may miss the novel insights and creative ideas that citizens frequently bring to the table.
- **Example:** participatory platforms have brought to light innovative urban solutions, such brand-new parks and neighborhood initiatives.

### 13.2.3.5. Cost-Effectiveness and Efficiency:

- Allocating resources in a more effective and efficient manner can result from crowdsourcing suggestions and comments.
- **Example:** through participatory budgeting, money is allocated to initiatives that have garnered the support of the general public.

### 13.2.4. Difficulties in Implementing Participatory Platforms

### 13.2.4.1. Digital Divide:

- Granting all individuals, even those without dependable internet connectivity or low digital literacy, equal access to participatory platforms.
- **Example:** other ways to participate, such internet-connected community centers or public kiosks, must be offered by urban designers.

### 13.2.4.2. Making Certain Meaningful Participation:

- Avoiding tokenistic methods and making sure that public participation truly influences decisions.
- **Example:** the regular publication of updates on the application of public input to foster involvement and trust.

### 13.2.4.3. Handling Huge Data Volumes:

- Processing and evaluating vast amounts of public information effectively in order to arrive at well-informed conclusions.

- **Example:** Classifying and ranking citizen suggestions using AI and machine learning.

### 13.2.4.4. Preserving Confidentiality and Security:

- Ensuring secure participation and safeguarding personal data to promote platform confidence.
- **Example:** Putting in place stringent data governance guidelines and end-to-end encryption are two examples.

### 13.2.4.5. Maintaining Involvement:

- Preventing participation fatigue and maintaining public engagement over time.
- **Example:** consistent feedback loops and platform updates with new features can support long-term engagement.

### 13.2.5. Techniques for Effective Implementation:

### 13.2.5.1. Outreach and Education:

- Launching initiatives to inform the public about the advantages of involvement and the proper way to utilize the platform.
- **Example:** community gatherings, seminars, and workshops can be used to present and describe the platform.

### 13.2.5.2. User-Focused Design:

- Including users in the design process to make sure the platform is user-friendly and fits their demands.
- **Example:** hold usability testing sessions with various user groups to get input and make adjustments.

### 13.2.5.3. Collaborations:

- Working together to support and promote the platform with partners in the commercial sector, educational institutions, and nonprofit organizations.
- **Example:** collaborating with academic institutions to carry out studies and enhance the platform using their findings.

### 13.2.5.4. Pilot Initiatives:

- Prior to a full-scale launch, pilot programs should be used to evaluate the platform and make any necessary improvements.
- **Example:** Starting a citywide participatory budgeting initiative after proving successful in a particular district.

### 13.2.5.5. Constant Enhancement:

- Modifying the platform frequently in response to user input and developments in technology.
- **Example:** A case in point would be the adoption of an iterative development method that integrates novel technology capabilities and continuous user feedback.

In summary, citizens' participatory platforms are effective instruments for boosting community-driven innovation, increasing democratic involvement, and increasing transparency. Your involvement in the development, implementation, and upkeep of these platforms is essential as an IT and urban planning specialist. Through tackling issues like the digital divide, guaranteeing significant involvement, and upholding security and privacy, you may contribute to the development of efficient participatory systems that enhance urban governance and empower residents. By utilizing strategic implementation approaches and referencing effective models, you can aid in the creation of cities that are more dynamic, inclusive, and responsive.

## 13.3. Enhancing Transparency and Accountability

Building public trust, strengthening governance, and encouraging an informed and involved citizenry all depend on increasing transparency and accountability in government and urban planning. Using cutting-edge techniques and technology as an IT and urban planning specialist can greatly help achieve these objectives. In-depth techniques and case studies of improving accountability and transparency in urban planning and governance will be covered in this talk.

13.3.1. **Important Ideas:**

13.3.1.1. **Transparency:**

- Transparency in public administration, enabling citizens to obtain information and comprehend the decision-making process.
- **Example:** posting comprehensive city finances online for public inspection.

13.3.1.2. **Accountability:**

- Holding institutions and government representatives accountable for their deeds and choices, making sure they adhere to moral, legal, and public standards.

- **Example:** Putting in place performance dashboards to monitor the advancement of government programs and initiatives is one example.

### 13.3.2. Strategies for Improving Accountability and Transparency

### 13.3.2.1. Open Data Projects:

- Granting the general public access to government data so they can utilize, evaluate, and exchange information.
- **Example:** The Open Government Data Platform in India provides datasets on a range of topics related to government, such as environmental statistics and public services.

### 13.3.2.2. E-Government Workspaces:

- Digital platforms that make it easier to obtain information, services, and tools for public involvement from the government.
- **Example:** By making government information and services readily available online, Estonia's e-governance system—which offers services like e-tax, e-residency, and e-health—improves openness.

### 13.3.2.3. Engaging Platforms:

- Instruments that let people take part in decision-making so their opinions are heard and taken into account.
- **Example:** The Decidim platform in Barcelona promotes open decision-making by empowering residents to participate in planning, budgeting, and policy-making.

### 13.3.2.4. Dashboards for Performance:

- Online dashboards that provide real-time updates and performance metrics while tracking and displaying the status of government activities and projects.
- **Example:** The City of Boston's CityScore dashboard tracks important performance indicators like the effectiveness of service delivery and emergency response times.

### 13.3.2.5. Public Forums and Consultations:

- Involving the public in town hall meetings, internet forums, and public consultations to get feedback on projects and policy.
- **Example:** the UK's Planning Portal ensures public participation in decisions on urban growth by enabling residents to examine and comment on planning applications.

### 13.3.2.6. Blockchain Technology:

- Securing and validating government documents, transactions, and procedures using blockchain technology to guarantee data integrity and openness.
- **Example:** The Republic of Georgia records property transactions in a transparent and impenetrable manner by using blockchain technology for land register.

13.3.2.7. **Mechanisms for Audit and Oversight:**

- Putting in place impartial audit and supervision organizations to keep an eye on government operations and guarantee adherence to legal requirements.
- **Example:** to guarantee government accountability and openness, the U.S. Government Accountability Office (GAO) carries out audits and investigations.

13.3.3. **Examples of Initiatives in the Transparency and Accountability Space**

13.3.3.1. **E-Government of Estonia**

- **Overview:** With its e-government platform, Estonia provides a plethora of e-services, making it a leader in digital governance.
- **Transparency:** People have internet access to public records, government services, and decision-making processes.
- **Accountability:** Public servants are held responsible for their decisions and actions by the system's accessibility and transparency.

13.3.3.2. **Open Government Partnerships (OGP):**

- **Overview:** A multilateral project designed to get governments to make firm promises to fight corruption, empower citizens, encourage transparency, and use new technologies.
- **Impact:** By releasing public contracts and establishing open data portals, participating nations create action plans to improve accountability and transparency.

13.3.3.3. **The Open Data Portal for New York City:**

- **Overview:** Datasets created by several city agencies are made available to the public through NYC Open Data.
- **Transparency:** Gives people the ability to examine data on subjects like education, public safety, and transportation.
- **Accountability:** By using the data, citizens and watchdog groups can make government agencies answerable for their actions and choices.

### 13.3.3.4. Brazil's Portal for Transparency:

- **Overview:** A website that offers comprehensive data on public spending and budget distribution.
- **Transparency:** The public can monitor public spending and learn how their money is being spent.
- **Accountability:** By making financial information available to the public, accountability improves oversight and lowers potential for corruption.

### 13.3.3.5. The Anti-Corruption and Civil Rights Commission (ACRC) of South Korea:

- **Overview:** The Clean Portal, run by ACRC, enables citizens to report corruption and track actions taken by the government.
- **Transparency:** Makes information about situations that have been reported and government actions available.
- **Accountability:** Encourages a culture of accountability by making sure that reported issues are investigated and resolved.

### 13.3.4. Role of Urban Planning in Increased Accountability and Transparency

### 13.3.4.1. Transparent Planning Procedures:

- Publicly reviewing and commenting on development projects, zoning laws, and comprehensive urban planning.
- **Example:** the planning department of the City of Toronto frequently releases planning documents and hosts open houses for suggested developments.

### 13.3.4.2. Participation of the Community:

- Using online surveys, public hearings, and participatory workshops to involve local people in planning decisions.
- **Example:** To ensure that development reflects public objectives, San Francisco's Participatory Budgeting program gives citizens the opportunity to suggest and vote on local projects.

### 13.3.4.3. Tools for Mapping and GIS:

- Urban data and planning projects are shown using Geographic Information Systems (GIS), which makes information more comprehensible and accessible.
- **Example:** to improve openness in municipal administration, the City of Chicago's Open Data Portal has interactive maps that display information on public health, building permits, and crime.

### 13.3.4.4. Systems for Tracking and Reporting:

- Putting in place mechanisms to track and report on the development of urban initiatives and legal compliance.
- **Example:** The City of Los Angeles promotes accountability and openness in urban development by using an online portal to monitor the status of building projects and code enforcement operations.

### 13.3.5.        Problems and Solutions

### 13.3.5.1. Security and Privacy of Data:

- Ensuring that efforts to promote openness don't jeopardize sensitive data or individual privacy.
- **Solution:** Enforcing stringent data security protocols and pre-anonymizing confidential information for publishing.

### 13.3.5.2. Digital Divide

- Ensuring that everyone can engage in transparency initiatives by having access to digital platforms and the internet.
- **Solution:** Offering digital literacy training and setting up public access sites like libraries and community centers.

### 13.3.5.3. Opposition to Change:

- Overcoming opposition to adopting transparent techniques from government employees and agencies.
- **Solution:** One potential solution is to offer government personnel incentives and training to encourage them to adopt accountability and transparency initiatives.

### 13.3.5.4. Data Integrity and Quality:

- Ensuring that data that is published is correct, current, and formatted consistently.
- **Solution:** The establishment of data governance frameworks and routine audits to ensure data quality are the solutions.

In summary, increasing accountability and openness in urban planning and governance is crucial to building public confidence, enhancing decision-making, and encouraging civic engagement. Using cutting-edge techniques and technology as an IT and urban planning specialist can greatly help achieve these objectives. You may contribute to the development of a more open and accountable government by putting policies like open data projects, e-government platforms, participatory tools, and strong oversight procedures into practice. You may create and put into place processes that guarantee individuals are aware, involved, and empowered to take part in community governance by drawing on effective models from around the globe.

# Chapter 14: Addressing Challenges and Ethical Considerations

## 14.1. Privacy and Data Security Concerns

Urban planning and IT both have serious privacy and data security issues, especially as cities grow increasingly digitally connected and dependent. I'll go over each of these issues in more detail below, with pertinent examples.

### 14.1.1. **Privacy Concerns:**

#### 14.1.1.1. **Monitoring and Surveillance**

- **Example:** Large-scale surveillance systems are frequently installed in smart cities to keep an eye on traffic, deter crime, and oversee public services. To improve public safety, London, for example, has a vast network of CCTV cameras. Nevertheless, since constant observation might result in abuse or overreach, this kind of surveillance may violate people's privacy.

- **Concern:** Surveillance data may be utilized for purposes other than those intended, thereby violating civil and personal liberties. The worry is that monitoring could result in a surveillance state where people are always under observation.

#### 14.1.1.2. **Collection and Usage of Data**

- **Example:** Homes with smart meters gather comprehensive data on energy use that can be used to improve energy use. Nevertheless, these data might also highlight trends regarding people's daily schedules, times at home, and lifestyle preferences.

- **Concern:** Without the individuals' express authorization, the aggregation of such data may result in profiling and unapproved sharing with marketers or insurance firms.

#### 14.1.1.3. **Tracking Location**

- **Example:** Location-based services (LBS) are frequently used in urban planning projects to enhance public transportation and lessen traffic. Applications that track users' positions and provide real-time updates and route improvements include Google Maps and apps for public transportation.

- **Concern:** An extensive record of people's whereabouts may result from ongoing location tracking. This information could be exploited for theft, stalking, or other nefarious purposes if it ends up in the wrong hands.

### 14.1.2. Data Security Concerns:

### 14.1.2.1. Cybersecurity Threats:

- **Example:** In 2021, fuel supplies throughout the East Coast were affected by a ransomware attack on Colonial Pipeline, a significant petroleum pipeline operator in the United States. These kinds of attacks draw attention to weak points in vital infrastructure.
- **Concerns:** Urban networks are becoming more interconnected, so a breach in one area might have a domino effect across the whole city. Threats to cybersecurity can result in the loss of important data, interruptions to services, and even bodily injury.

### 14.1.2.2. Data Breaches:

- **Example:** the 2017 Equifax data breach revealed the personal details of over 147 million individuals, including names, addresses, birth dates, Social Security numbers, and, in certain situations, driver's license numbers.
- **Concerns** Sensitive information can be stolen as a result of data breaches, which can cause identity theft, monetary loss, and reputational harm. If resident data is corrupted in urban planning, it could damage public confidence and impede future developments.

### 14.1.2.3. Vulnerability of Interconnected Systems

- **Example:** consider the growing interconnectivity of electricity grids, water management systems, and smart traffic signals. A cyberattack on Israel's water infrastructure in 2020 sought to contaminate the water supply by changing chemical concentrations.
- **Concerns:** A vulnerability in one region may expose others due to the interconnected nature of smart city technologies. It is extremely difficult to guarantee system security, and a single network component failure might have far-reaching effects.

### 14.1.3. Reducing Data Security and Privacy Issues

### 14.1.3.1. Rules and Guidelines

- **Example:** The European Union's General Data Protection Regulation (GDPR) establishes stringent restrictions for the collection, storage, and use of personal data. It offers a strong framework for data protection and privacy.
- **Solution:** Similar laws may be put in place at the local level to guarantee responsible data handling and to provide explicit rules for consent, usage, and personal information protection.

### 14.1.3.2. Data Anonymization and Encryption

- **Example:** Sensitive data can be shielded from unwanted access by using encryption algorithms during data transit and storage. Techniques for data anonymization can guarantee that personal information cannot be linked to specific people.
- **Solution:** To preserve residents' privacy and also get the benefits of data analytics, cities should implement robust encryption standards and anonymize data whenever feasible.

### 14.1.3.3. Public Participation and Awareness:

- **Example:** involving the public in conversations regarding data security and privacy can serve to foster confidence and guarantee that laws represent community concerns. Residents of Barcelona can take part in decision-making processes, particularly those pertaining to data policies, through the Decidim portal.
- **Resolution:** To guarantee that privacy concerns are addressed and locals feel more confident about the data, transparent communication and public participation in the establishment and execution of data regulations are essential.

In summary, data security and privacy are critical factors to take into account when integrating IT with urban planning. Cities may take advantage of technology while safeguarding the security and privacy of their citizens by putting strong security measures in place, following rules, and involving the public.

## 14.2. Overcoming the Digital Divide

IT and urban planning professionals face a significant challenge in bridging the digital gap, which exacerbates social inequality and impedes fair access to opportunities and services. The difference in access to contemporary information and communication technology (ICT) between those with and without it is known as the "*digital divide*." I'll go over some strategies for closing the digital divide below, with where applicable examples.

### 14.2.1. **Strategies to Bridge the Digital Divide**

#### 14.2.1.1. **Infrastructure Development:**

- **Example:** In the US, Google Fiber is one example.
- **Context:** By constructing a fiber-optic network, Google Fiber hopes to offer high-speed internet access in a number of American communities. Gigabit internet speeds are provided by this infrastructure, which are far faster than typical broadband rates.
- **Solution:** Infrastructure spending is essential. *Broadband network expansion is a joint venture between governments and private enterprises, especially in underserved urban and rural areas.* This may entail installing satellite internet in far-off areas, improving mobile networks, and installing fiber-optic connections.

#### 14.2.1.2. **Community and Public Wi-Fi Access Points**

- **Example:** NYC LinkNYC Project, for instance.
- **Context:** LinkNYC is an initiative that uses kiosks placed throughout New York City to offer free public Wi-Fi. In addition, these kiosks provide access to city services, phone calls, and device charging.
- **Resolution:** For those who cannot afford home internet access, *public Wi-Fi hotspots and community internet access points can be established in parks, libraries, community centers, and other public locations.* By doing this, it is guaranteed that all locals may access crucial internet resources.

#### 14.2.1.3. **Programs for Affordable Access**

- **Example:** Comcast Internet Essentials, for instance.
- **Context:** Low-income American households can now afford internet access thanks to Comcast's Internet Essentials program. The program offers discounted broadband access, subsidized PCs, and training in digital literacy.
- **Solution:** One potential solution to lower financial barriers is to *implement affordable access programs that give economically disadvantaged groups access to low-cost internet services and devices.* The sustainability of these programs can be increased through partnerships and subsidies with internet service providers (ISPs).

14.2.1.4. **Training in Digital Literacy:**
- **Example:** UK Online Centers.
- **Context:** To help people become more digitally literate, the UK Online Centers network offers training in digital skills. These centers provide low-cost or free computer, internet, and software application training sessions.
- **Solution:** To guarantee that people have access to technology and are proficient with it, *digital literacy initiatives are crucial.* These programs, which cater to various age groups and ability levels, can be made available through community centers, libraries, schools, and internet platforms.

14.2.1.5. **Smart City and Inclusive Urban Planning Initiatives**
- **Example:** Barcelona's Smart City Strategy, for instance.
- **Context:** Using technology to ensure inclusivity while improving urban living circumstances is the main goal of Barcelona's smart city concept. To improve public services like waste collection, traffic control, and smart lighting, the city uses a variety of ICT solutions, making sure that everyone can take advantage of these advantages.
- **Solution:** Digital inclusion should be incorporated into smart city projects by urban planners. This entails *creating public services and infrastructure that are available to all citizens, even those from underserved communities.* Cities can guarantee that technological improvements benefit everyone by emphasizing inclusive design.

14.2.1.6. **Collaborative Efforts and Partnerships**
- **Example:** The Kansas City-based Digital Inclusion Alliance.
- **Context:** To combat the digital divide, local businesses, government agencies, and groups have joined together to form the Kansas City Digital Inclusion Alliance. They concentrate on projects like increasing broadband availability, supplying reasonably priced gadgets, and providing instruction in digital literacy.
- **Solution:** To bridge the digital divide completely, *collaborations between the public and corporate sectors, non-profits, and community organizations can pool resources and knowledge.* Working together can result in more extensive and successful outcomes.

14.2.1.7. **Advocacy and Policy:**

- **Example:** The European Union's Digital Agenda for Europe.
- **Context:** Ensuring that European citizens profit from digital breakthroughs is the goal of the Digital Agenda for Europe program. It contains measures to broaden the reach of broadband, encourage digital literacy, and guarantee that digital services are available to all.
- **Solution:** One potential solution to promote digital inclusion is for *governments to implement laws requiring cheap internet access, subsidizing digital infrastructure, and requiring participation in digital literacy initiatives.* Prioritizing digital inclusion on public agendas can be achieved through advocacy at the local and national levels.

In summary, a multimodal strategy that combines partnerships, cheap access initiatives, digital literacy training, inclusive urban design, infrastructure development, and supportive legislation is needed to close the digital gap. Through the implementation of these policies, cities may promote social inclusion and economic opportunity by guaranteeing that all inhabitants have fair access to the advantages of the digital era.

In order to ensure a more inclusive and connected society, urban planners and IT specialists are essential to this endeavor because they can create and execute solutions that bridge the divide between the digitally connected and the disconnected.

## 14.3. Ethical Use of AI and Technology

To make sure that technological breakthroughs serve society as a whole and do not create harm or worsen already-existing inequities, ethical usage of AI and technology in urban planning and IT is crucial. Fairness, openness, privacy, accountability, and the effects of technology on society are all ethical factors to take into account. I'll go into further detail about each of these topics below, citing instances as appropriate.

### 14.3.1. **Non-Discrimination and Impartial:**
- **Example:** AI in Policing
- **Context:** Artificial intelligence (AI) is used by predictive policing systems to evaluate data and forecast crime scenes. However, because these systems frequently rely on past crime data that may reflect discriminatory policing methods, they have come under fire for perpetuating preexisting biases.

- **Solution:** AI systems need to be developed and trained on a variety of representative datasets in order to guarantee fairness. *It is the active responsibility of developers and policymakers to detect and address biases in AI algorithms.* Furthermore, it is imperative to conduct periodic audits and assessments to guarantee that AI systems do not disproportionately affect particular populations.

## 14.3.2. Explainability and Transparency

- **Example:** Algorithmic Decision-Making in Urban Services,
- **Context:** Urban services like figuring out who qualifies for social programs or streamlining traffic are using AI algorithms more and more. The lives of the citizens may be greatly impacted by these choices, yet the algorithms' inner workings are frequently unclear.
- **Solution:** AI systems must be transparent. This implies that the public should be able to comprehend and clearly understand the standards and reasoning that underlie algorithmic judgments. *Explainability tools can be used to aid deconstruct decision-making processes, and disclosure of information regarding AI systems used by public agencies need to be mandatory.*

## 14.3.3. Data Protection and Privacy

- **Example:** Smart City Sensors
- **Context:** To gather information on everything from traffic patterns to air quality, smart cities use a variety of sensors and Internet of Things devices. Although this data might enhance urban administration, improper handling of it may result in privacy invasions for people.
- **Solution:** To safeguard people's privacy, data gathered via smart city *technology needs to be encrypted and anonymized.* For data collection, storage, and use, clear policies and standards must be created in order to comply with privacy laws like GDPR. Citizens ought to be aware of how their data is used and have control over it.

## 14.3.4. Governance and Accountability

- **Example:** Autonomous vehicles, for instance
- **Context:** A number of cities are testing and deploying autonomous vehicles (AVs). Accidents involving AVs raise concerns about liability and accountability even though they promise better safety and efficiency.

- **Resolution:** Resilient governance mechanisms are required to handle technology and AI accountability. *The obligations of AI system developers, operators, and users should be clearly outlined in rules.* In order to rectify any harm produced by AI technologies, mechanisms for accountability and reparation need be in place.

### 14.3.5. Impact on Society and Inclusion

- **Example:** AI in Urban Planning, for Example
- **Context:** Planning for public transportation, infrastructure development, and zoning are just a few of the urban planning procedures that AI may streamline. But there's a chance that new technologies will put efficiency ahead of equity, which might push vulnerable populations to the margins.
- **Solution:** IT experts and urban planners should make sure that the application of AI technologies is in line with more general social objectives, such sustainability and inclusion. *Community participation and participatory planning processes can assist ensure that the advantages of AI are dispersed equally and that the interests of all citizens are considered.*

### 14.3.6. Comprehensive Plans for the Ethical Application of Technology and AI

1. **Ethical Guidelines and Frameworks**
   - **Example:** The IEEE Global Initiative on Ethics of Autonomous and Intelligent Systems offers thorough recommendations for the moral development and application of AI.
   - **Solution:** Governments and organizations should *establish and abide by ethical standards that direct the creation and application of AI.* These frameworks ought to tackle matters such as equity, responsibility, and openness, including specific directives for professionals.

### 14.3.7. Development and Design that is Inclusive

- **Example:** diversified teams of ethicists, sociologists, and representatives from impacted communities ought to be involved in the development of AI systems.
- **Solution:** The use of inclusive design techniques guarantees that AI systems *take into account the demands and values of a wide range of users.* Early identification of potential ethical difficulties during the design and development process might be facilitated by involving stakeholders from diverse backgrounds.

### 14.3.8. Constant Observation and Assessment

- **Example:** the implementation of AI systems should incorporate procedures for continuing observation and analysis in order to gauge their effects and spot any moral dilemmas.
- **Solution:** To *make sure AI systems stay compliant with ethical standards, feedback loops and frequent audits should be put in place.* Ongoing assessment enables modifications and enhancements to tackle any new problems.

In summary, to create just, open, and inclusive systems, ethical AI and technology use is crucial in both IT and urban planning. We can minimize potential risks while maximizing the benefits of AI and technology by following ethical norms, maintaining responsibility and openness, safeguarding privacy, and taking the influence on society into account. Urban planners and IT specialists may guarantee that technological improvements contribute positively to society and support the well-being of all citizens by means of deliberate design, effective governance, and continuous review.

# Chapter 15: Case Studies of Leading Smart Cities

## 15.1. Nashville (Tennessee): Sustainable Development

The quality of life, sustainability, and municipal operations have all significantly improved as a result of IoT implementation in urban management. The following provides in-depth analyses of effective IoT deployments in numerous global cities:

The Reasons Chattanooga Is Listed as a Smart City:

a. **Internet via Gigabit:** Chattanooga is renowned for having developed *the first high-speed internet network*. With the installation of one of the first gigabit-speed internet networks in the US, the city-owned Electric Power Board (EPB) gained the moniker "*Gig City.*" From sophisticated manufacturing to telemedicine, this infrastructure serves a range of applications related to smart cities.

b. **Smart Grid Technology:** To improve energy efficiency and dependability, the EPB has deployed a smart grid. The automated metering infrastructure (AMI) and sensors in this system help control and minimize power outages, increasing the power distribution network's overall efficiency.

c. **Sustainability Initiatives:** Chattanooga has made investments in energy-efficient buildings, large green areas, and improved public transit as part of its commitment to sustainable urban development. A crucial component of the city's smart city concept is its emphasis on sustainability.

## 15.2. Paris (France): Pioneering Sustainable Development

The Reasons Paris Is Listed as a Smart City:

a. **Sustainable Mobility:** Paris is renowned for its creative approaches to mobility, like the Autolib electric car-sharing scheme and the Vélib bike-sharing system. To lessen pollution and traffic, the city has also invested in large bike lanes and pedestrian zones.

b. **Energy Efficiency:** Through programs like the *Paris Climate Action Plan*, which includes adapting buildings for renewable energy, Paris has committed to lowering its carbon footprint.

c. **Smart Waste Management:** In order to increase efficiency and lessen its impact on the environment, Paris has installed smart rubbish bins that are fitted with sensors to track fill levels and optimize collection routes.

d. **Citizen Engagement:** Paris involves the public in urban planning and decision-making processes by using digital platforms. By allowing citizens to suggest and decide on civic initiatives, the *"Madame Mayor, I Have an Idea"* campaign promotes a participatory style of government.

## 15.3. Zhejiang Province (China): Pioneering Technological Advancement

The Reasons Zhejiang Is Listed as a Smart City Region:

a. **Digital Infrastructure:** Zhejiang is renowned for its cutting-edge digital infrastructure, which includes broad use of IoT devices and substantial 5G coverage. Its capital, Hangzhou, is especially well-known for this. Alibaba, a multinational technology company based in Hangzhou, has made a substantial contribution to the technical progress of the area.

b. **Smart Transportation:** To improve traffic flow and lessen congestion, Hangzhou has put in place a smart traffic management system that makes use of big data and artificial intelligence. The city also has a robust public transit system, which includes smart bus and high-speed rail.

c. **Smart Governance:** To improve efficiency and transparency, the Zhejiang government has embraced digital platforms for governance. Data analytics is used by programs like Hangzhou's "City Brain" project to enhance public services, including traffic control and healthcare.

d. **Economic Development**: With a large number of tech parks and incubators that assist start-ups and tech enterprises, Zhejiang is a center for innovation and entrepreneurship. The development of smart city solutions is being driven by this innovation focus in a number of sectors.

## 15.4. Barcelona (Spain): Smart City Infrastructure:

a. **Overview:** Barcelona is frequently mentioned as a model smart city that uses IoT technology to improve urban management and lifestyle.

b. **Important Implementations:**
   o **Smart Lighting:**

- **Description:** Streetlights in Barcelona are equipped with Internet of Things capabilities, which allow them to modify their brightness in response to the presence of cars and people.
        - **Benefits:** This helps achieve sustainability goals by reducing light pollution and energy usage by about 30%.
    - **Smart Parking**:
        - **Description**: The city uses Internet of Things (IoT) sensors in parking spots to track availability and direct cars to open spots through a mobile app.
        - **Benefits:** By reducing pollutants, this improves air quality and lessens traffic congestion brought on by drivers looking for parking.
    - **Environmental Monitoring:**
        - **Description**: IoT sensors are used across the city to track humidity, noise levels, and air quality.
        - **Benefits:** City officials may make well-informed judgments on urban development and public health thanks to real-time data. Additionally, available to the public, the data encourages openness and involvement in the community.

c. **Results:** Barcelona's all-encompassing strategy for integrating IoT has improved public services, managed traffic more effectively, and reduced energy consumption, making it a global leader in smart city development.

## 15.5. Singapore: Smart Nation Initiative:

a. **Overview:** The goal of Singapore's Smart Nation effort is to use technology to enhance urban living, spur economic development, and build stronger community ties.

b. **Important Implementations:**
    - **Smart Transportation:**
        - **Description:** Singapore uses an advanced IoT-enhanced public transportation system. Commuters can use smartphone apps to access real-time information on the whereabouts of

buses and trains, the number of passengers, and the arrival timings.
- **Benefits:** This enhances the commuting experience overall, cuts down on waiting times, and optimizes transit timetables.
- **Water Resources Management:**
  - **Description:** The city-state has implemented intelligent water meters that offer current information on water consumption and identify potential leaks.
  - **Benefits:** This assures effective management of the water supply, lowers waste, and promotes water conservation.
- **Smart Homes:**
  - **Description:** IoT sensors are installed in housing complexes to track rubbish collection, energy use, and even the wellbeing of the residents.
  - **Benefits:** By using non-intrusive health monitoring, this improves sustainability, makes living environments more comfortable, and aids in the care of the aged.

c. **Results:** Singapore's Smart Nation project serves as an example of how a unified, national IoT strategy may improve urban administration and the standard of living for its citizens.

## 15.6. London (UK): Smart Traffic Management:

a. **Overview:** To solve its serious pollution and traffic congestion problems, London has deployed a number of IoT technologies.

b. **Important Implementations:**
- **Monitoring Traffic in Real Time:**
  - **Description:** The city's IoT sensors and cameras gather information on vehicle speeds, traffic patterns, and areas of congestion.
  - **Benefits:** By utilizing this data to optimize traffic signal timings and give drivers real-time traffic updates, traffic congestion is decreased and travel times are shortened.
- **Congestion Charging:**

- **Description:** The congestion charge zone in London employs Internet of Things (IoT) technology to track vehicle arrivals and impose appropriate fees on drivers.
        - **Benefits:** By successfully reducing the number of vehicles in downtown London, this has lowered pollution and promoted public transportation use.
    - **Monitoring of Air Quality:**
        - **Description:** Real-time data on pollution levels throughout the city is provided by Internet of Things-enabled air quality sensors.
        - **Benefits:** By providing residents with information about air quality and helping the city execute pollution reduction initiatives, this information especially benefits those who have respiratory ailments.
- **c. Results:** By utilizing IoT for traffic and environmental management, London has demonstrated the potential of IoT in big, complex cities by reducing traffic, improving air quality, and improving urban mobility.

## 15.7. New York City (USA): Smart Water Management

- **a. Overview:** With an emphasis on sustainability and efficiency, New York City has implemented Internet of Things technology to improve its water management system.
- **b. Important Implementations:**
    - **Automated Meter Reading (AMR):**
        - **Description:** The city has fitted water meters with AMR devices, which wirelessly send usage information to a central database.
        - **Benefits** include the elimination of human meter reading, a decrease in inaccurate billing, and speedy leak and anomalous usage pattern detection.
    - **Smart Irrigation:**
        - **Description:** IoT-enabled irrigation systems in parks and public areas modify watering schedules in response to current meteorological information.

- **Benefits:** This ensures healthy green spaces even during drought situations and maximizes the use of water resources.

c. **Results:** New York City's smart water management programs have increased the sustainability of its water delivery system, decreased operating expenses, and optimized resource efficiency.

## 15.8. Amsterdam (Netherlands): Smart Waste Management:

a. **Overview:** One of the main initiatives the city is taking to become a more sustainable city is the implementation of a smart waste management system.

b. **Important Implementations:**
   - **Smart Bins:**
     - **Description:** Real-time waste buildup monitoring is provided by IoT-enabled waste bins with fill-level sensors.
     - **Benefits:** By allowing for optimum collection routes, garbage collection vehicles' fuel consumption and emissions are decreased.
   - **Recycling Monitoring:**
     - **Description:** Recycling containers are equipped with sensors that monitor the kinds and amounts of items gathered.
     - **Benefits:** By educating residents about their recycling behaviors and recycling rates, this data promotes better waste segregation methods.

c. **Results:** By lowering operating expenses, increasing recycling rates, and improving waste collection efficiency, Amsterdam's smart waste management system has helped the city achieve its sustainability objectives.

# Examples of Smart Cities

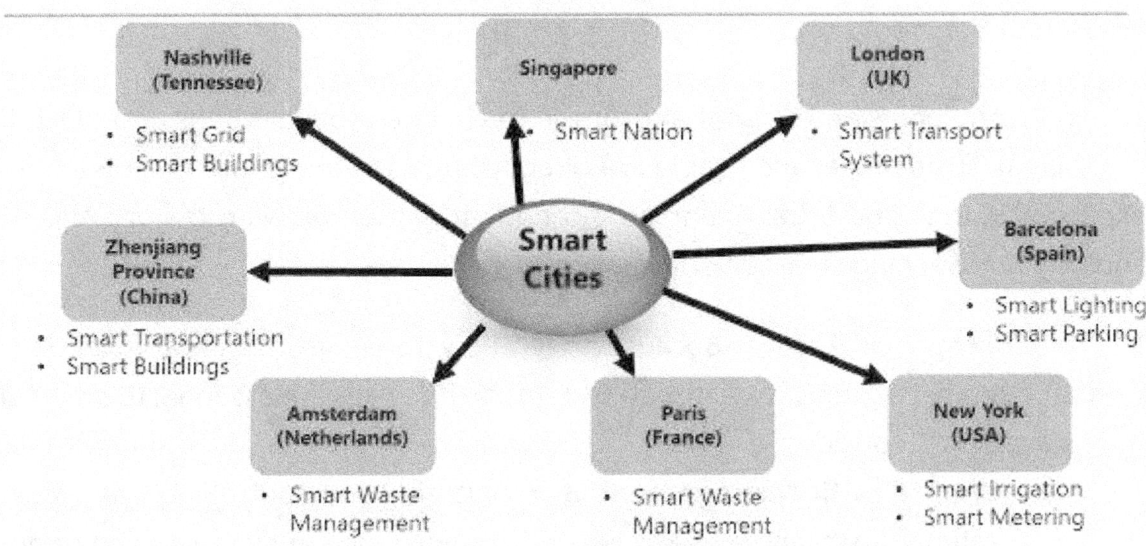


**Source:** Smart Cities: *The Technology Transforming Urban Living;* GoodMan Series, (Patrick Mukosha, 2024).

*Figure 9: Examples of Smart Cities*

In summary, these case studies demonstrate how the Internet of Things is revolutionizing urban administration in a number of areas, such as waste management, electricity, water, transportation, and environmental monitoring. Cities like Barcelona, Singapore, London, New York City, and Amsterdam have improved their citizens' quality of life, sustainability, and efficiency by utilizing IoT technologies. Other cities hoping to grow smarter and more resilient in the face of urbanization and global concerns should take inspiration from these well-executed models.

A variety of characteristics, such as cutting-edge digital infrastructure, sustainable practices, intelligent transportation systems, and public involvement programs, are exemplified by each of these cities and areas. They may take different techniques and concentrate on different topics, but they all use technology to increase efficiency, encourage sustainability, and improve urban living. These cities are leading the smart city movement, whether it is via their innovative high-speed internet (Chattanooga), broad digital integration (Zhejiang), comprehensive data platforms (London), or sustainable mobility solutions (Paris).

# Chapter 16: The Future of Smart Cities

## 16.1. Emerging Technologies and Innovations

Emerging technologies and ideas that promise to change urban settings and make them more efficient, sustainable, and livable are directly linked to the future of smart cities. As an expert in both IT and urban planning, I can identify the following major areas where technology is advancing smart city development:

16.1.1. **The Internet of Things**: Because they allow for real-time data collection and management across several urban systems, IoT devices are essential to smart cities. As examples, consider:

    a. **Smart Traffic Management:** By monitoring and controlling traffic flow, *IoT sensors installed in roadways and traffic signals may ease congestion and boost safety*. Barcelona, for example, has IoT-enabled traffic lights that react instantly to changes in vehicle and pedestrian traffic.

    b. **Smart Waste Management:** By optimizing collection routes and monitoring fill levels, *sensors installed in waste bins lower operating costs and pollutants*. This is demonstrated by the smart trash management system in Singapore, which minimizes needless collection visits.

16.1.2. **Machine Learning (ML) And Artificial Intelligence (AI):** In order to analyze and forecast the massive volumes of data created by IoT devices, Artificial Intelligence (AI) and Machine Learning (ML) are essential.

    a. **Predictive Maintenance:** *AI can identify when expensive malfunctions in infrastructure, such as water pipes or bridges, are necessary*. AI-driven analytics, for instance, assist in monitoring and maintaining infrastructure and water quality in Los Angeles.

    b. **Smart Policing:** As demonstrated by Chicago's predictive policing initiative, AI algorithms examine crime trends to more wisely deploy police resources.

16.1.3. **5G Connectivity**: Faster and more dependable internet connections are made possible by 5G technology, which is essential for the real-time data sharing that smart cities demand.

    a. **Improved Public Services:** *5G makes it possible for emergency services to communicate quickly and efficiently, which improves coordination and reaction times.*

b. **Autonomous Vehicles:** *5G is necessary for the deployment of autonomous vehicles in order to provide real-time connectivity with other vehicles and infrastructure.* 5G networks are being tested in cities like Tokyo to enable driverless cabs.

16.1.4. **Blockchain:** Transparent and safe transaction records offered by blockchain boost efficiency and confidence in a range of urban applications.

a. **Land Registration:** By streamlining land registry procedures, *blockchain can cut down on fraud and red tape.* By2025, all official documents should be stored on blockchain, according to Dubai's blockchain strategy.

b. **Energy Trading:** *Peer-to-peer energy trading is made possible by blockchain, enabling locals to purchase and sell extra renewable energy.* The innovative Brooklyn Microgrid in New York is one such instance.

16.1.5. **Smart Grids and Renewable Energy:** Smart grids and renewable energy sources are necessary for sustainable urban development.

a. **Microgrids:** By combining renewable energy sources and boosting resilience, these *smaller grids can function either separately or in tandem with the larger grid.* A microgrid run by the University of California, San Diego combines multiple renewable energy sources.

b. **Energy Management Systems:** *Optimize consumption and cut down on waste by balancing the supply and demand of energy through the use of AI and IoT.* These kinds of technology are used in Amsterdam's smart grid project to effectively incorporate renewable energy.

16.1.6. **Self-Driving Vehicles:** Urban mobility is about to undergo a radical change because to autonomous transportation systems, which include public transportation, cars, and drones.

a. **Self-Driving Buses:** To offer effective and adaptable public transportation, cities like Helsinki are testing autonomous buses.

b. **Drone Delivery:** Organizations such as Amazon are creating drone delivery systems that have the potential to lower pollution and traffic in cities.

16.1.7. **Smart Structures and Systems:** IoT and AI are used in smart buildings to increase tenant comfort, security, and energy efficiency.

a. **Energy-Efficient Buildings:** Depending on occupancy and meteorological conditions, buildings with smart sensor systems can modify lighting, heating, and cooling. Amsterdam's The Edge is a prime example of a clever, environmentally friendly structure.

b. **Infrastructure Monitoring:** By keeping an eye on the structural integrity of tunnels, bridges, and other infrastructure, Internet of Things sensors can identify maintenance needs in advance. Such technology is used on the UK's Severn Bridge.

16.1.8. **Platforms for Citizen Engagement:** These platforms use technology to engage the public in urban government and planning.

   a. **Participatory Budgeting:** Online platforms are used by cities such as Paris to allow citizens to cast votes on budget allocations for local initiatives.

   b. **Feedback Systems:** By enabling citizens to report problems to local governments directly, apps such as SeeClickFix promote a cooperative approach to urban administration.

16.1.9. **Monitoring of the Environment:** Urban sustainability is aided by the monitoring and management of environmental issues through advanced sensors and data analytics.

   a. **Air Quality Monitoring:** Big cities like Beijing have set up massive networks for monitoring air quality, giving locals access to data and forecasts in real time.

   b. **Water Management:** Israel's sophisticated water management system demonstrates how smart sensors and AI can more effectively manage water supplies.

In summary, the incorporation of these cutting-edge technology will enable the development of connected, effective, and sustainable urban environments—the future of smart cities. Cities may address the issues associated with urbanization and enhance the quality of life for their citizens by utilizing IoT, AI, 5G, blockchain, renewable energy, autonomous mobility, smart infrastructure, public participation, and environmental monitoring. These developments open the door for resilient and adaptable urban ecosystems by encouraging more environmental stewardship and community involvement in addition to improving operational efficiency.

## 16.2. Creating Resilient and Adaptive Cities

The development of robust and adaptable cities is essential to the success of smart cities in the future. The ability of a city to endure and bounce back from a variety of shocks and strains, including natural disasters, climate change, and economic ups and downs, is referred to as resilience. Adaptability is the ability to change with the times and apply lessons learned to enhance urban life. Here are several important tactics and tools that enhance the resilience and adaptability of smart cities, as demonstrated by actual cases from my experience as an IT and urban planning specialist:

16.2.1. **Data-Based Decision Making:**
- Through the use of big data and analytics, cities may make well-informed decisions that improve resilience.
- **Example:** The *Office of Emergency Management in New York City* employs data analytics to forecast and handle natural disasters like storms and flooding. The city's Advanced Warning System provides coordination and real-time notifications by integrating data from many sources.

16.2.2. **Smart Infrastructure:**
- Cities can monitor and address problems before they get out of hand by implementing AI and IoT sensors into their infrastructure.
- **Example:** The UK's *Severn Bridge* is outfitted with Internet of Things (IoT) sensors that continuously check the structural integrity of the structure, identifying any maintenance requirements and averting possible failures.

16.2.3. **Climate Resilient Designs:**
- Urban planning that incorporates climate-robust architecture makes cities more resilient to harsh weather occurrences.
- **Example:** *Rotterdam,* Netherlands, has created water plazas to reduce the risk of flooding by acting as entertainment areas in the dry months and as places to store water during seasons of high rainfall.

16.2.4. **Integration of Renewable Energy:**
- Sustainability and energy resilience are increased by using smart grids and renewable energy sources.
- **Example:** The *University of California,* San Diego runs a microgrid that combines biogas, wind, and solar energy to provide energy security and lessen reliance on the main grid in times of emergency.

16.2.5. **Ecological Infrastructure:**
- Parks, green roofs, and permeable pavements are examples of green infrastructure that helps cities manage storm water, lower the amount of urban heat islands, and enhance air quality.

- **Example:** Singapore's "*City in a Garden*" project combines large green areas with vertical gardens to improve urban living conditions and increase environmental resilience.

### 16.2.6. Community Involvement and Engagement:

- Involving the public in resilience and urban planning initiatives guarantees that the solutions are supported by the community and broadly embraced.
- **Example:** The *City of Paris* employs participatory budgeting to give citizens a voice in decision-making by letting them suggest and vote on initiatives that strengthen community resilience.

### 16.2.7. Systems for Disaster Preparedness and Response:

- Technology-enabled advanced systems for disaster preparedness and response guarantee prompt and efficient responses to crises.
- **Example:** *Tokyo* has established disaster preparedness measures that encompass early warning systems for seismic activity and tsunamis, thorough evacuation plans, and public education initiatives.

### 16.2.8. Adaptive Transportation Systems:

- Systems of transportation that are robust and flexible can adjust to shifting circumstances and maintain mobility even in the face of disruptions.
- **Example:** *Helsinki* is developing autonomous buses that can offer dependable, flexible transportation by modifying routes and schedules in response to demand and traffic conditions in real time.

### 16.2.9. Systems for Managing Water:

- In addition to minimizing waste and ensuring the availability of clean water, smart water management systems also monitor and optimize water usage.
- **Example:** the national water management system in Israel makes effective use of water in a water-scarce region by monitoring water quality, identifying leaks, and optimizing irrigation using cutting-edge sensors and data analytics.

### 16.2.10. Integration of Social Services and Health:

- Ensuring that vulnerable populations are supported during crises is made possible by integrating social and health services within the framework of smart cities.
- **Example:** The *Vincles BCN project* in Barcelona employs technology to link senior citizens with social workers and carers, therefore lowering isolation and guaranteeing prompt assistance in case of emergency.

16.2.11.    **Policies for Resilient Urban Planning**:

- Cities can better prepare for upcoming issues by creating and implementing resilient and adaptable urban planning strategies.
- **Example:** The *Climate Adaptation Plan for Copenhagen* outlines measures like elevated roadways and green roofs to absorb the effects of extreme rainfall and rising sea levels.

16.2.12.    **Diversification of the Economy**

- Encouraging economic diversification improves a city's economic resilience by reducing reliance on a single industry.
- **Example:** *Medellín, Colombia*, has improved its economic resilience by evolving from a textile-dependent city to a center for technology, education, and tourism.

16.2.13.    **Collaborative Ventures**

- Projects focusing on resilience and adaptation gain access to more resources and knowledge when they work with partners in the business sector.
- **Example:** The *Rockefeller Foundation's 100 Resilient Cities program* works with cities all around the world to create and implement resilience plans by utilizing public-private partnerships.

In summary, building systems that can endure and recover from a variety of shocks requires combining cutting-edge technologies, creative urban design techniques, and community involvement to create resilient and adaptive cities. Cities can improve their resilience and adaptability by utilizing data analytics, smart infrastructure, renewable energy, climate-resilient architecture, green infrastructure, and other tactics. Examples from actual cities, such as Tokyo, Singapore, Rotterdam, New York, and others, show how successful these strategies are in creating resilient, habitable, and sustainable urban environments.

## 16.3. Human-Centric Design in Urban Development

The planning, design, and management of cities should put people's needs, preferences, and well-being first. This is known as human-centric design in urban development. It entails developing livable, accessible, and inclusive urban areas with an emphasis on improving everyone's quality of life. Here are some essential elements of human-centric design in urban development, as demonstrated by actual cases, from the perspective of an IT and urban planning specialist:

### 16.3.1. **Accessible and Inclusive Urban Environments**:

- Everyone may enjoy and profit from the city's advantages when urban areas are designed to be inclusive and accessible to all, including the elderly, children, and those with disabilities.
- **Example:** The inclusive urban planning of *Curitiba*, Brazil, is well-known. The accessibility features of the city's bus rapid transit (BRT) system, like elevated platforms and low-floor buses, make it simple for the elderly and others with disabilities to use public transportation.

### 16.3.2. **Engagement with the Community and Public Participation:**

- Urban development that takes into account community needs and preferences is guaranteed when individuals are involved in the planning and decision-making stages.
- **Example:** Participatory budgeting was invented in *Porto Alegre*, Brazil, enabling locals to have direct control over the distribution of public expenditures. Many cities throughout the world have embraced this strategy, which encourages increased community involvement and guarantees that public investments take local needs into account.

### 16.3.3. **Mixed-Use Construction:**

- In addition to reducing the need for lengthy journeys, mixed-use complexes that bring together residential, commercial, and recreational spaces near together also promote lively, walkable districts.
- **Example:** Consider the mixed-use *Carlsberg Byen Development* in Copenhagen, which combines residential, commercial, retail, and cultural areas. By encouraging a sense of community and lowering dependency on automobiles, the project helps create a more sustainable urban environment.

### 16.3.4. **Open Areas and Greenery:**

- Urban areas that incorporate green and open spaces into their design provide places for socializing, relaxation, and recreation while also improving the physical and emotional well-being of its citizens.

- **Example:** *Central Park* in New York City is a model urban green space that provides millions of locals and tourists with a vital hub for social and recreational activities. It provides a break from the city.

### 16.3.5. **Sustainable and Eco-Friendly Design:**

- Using sustainable design ideas reduces urban development's negative environmental effects and encourages better living environments.
- **Example:** The eco-friendly *BedZED* (Beddington Zero Energy Development) housing project in London uses sustainable materials, renewable energy sources, and energy-efficient design. It provides as an example of how to lessen carbon footprints and encourage sustainable urban living.

### 16.3.6. **Smart Mobility Options:**

- Urban mobility is improved and pollution and traffic congestion are decreased by putting smart mobility solutions into place, such as integrated public transportation networks, bike-sharing programs, and electric vehicle charging stations.
- **Example:** *Amsterdam* is one of the world's most bike-friendly cities thanks to its robust bike-sharing program and well-developed bicycle infrastructure. This strategy not only lessens pollution and traffic jams but also encourages healthier lifestyles.

### 16.3.7. **Architecture at Human Scale**:

- A more intimate and interesting urban environment is produced when structures and public areas are designed at human scale as opposed to accommodating large-scale infrastructure and automobiles.
- **Example:** An abandoned rail line is the site of New York City's elevated linear park, known as *The High Line*. Its layout promotes socializing and strolling, resulting in a human-scale public area that draws both locals and visitors.

### 16.3.8. **Social Services and Infrastructure:**

- Maintaining sufficient social infrastructure in metropolitan areas, such as community centers, schools, and medical facilities, promotes the growth and well-being of locals.
- **Example:** To promote well-rounded communities, the *Housing and Development Board* (HDB) in Singapore makes sure that new residential developments are matched with the essential social infrastructure, such as parks, schools, and healthcare facilities.

16.3.9. **Integration of Culture and Art:**

- Urban designs that include cultural and artistic components are more aesthetically pleasing and help cities develop a feeling of identity and community.
- **Example:** see how art and culture have changed numerous public areas in *Medellín, Colombia*. The city's Biblioteca España is a cultural hub and library that has evolved into a representation of social change and neighborhood pride.

16.3.10. **Adaptable and Robust Design:**

- Long-term sustainability and resilience are ensured by designing urban areas that can adjust to changing requirements and circumstances, such as population expansion and climate change.
- **Example:** *Tokyo*'s urban planning incorporates elements that allow the city to adapt to a variety of difficulties, including earthquakes and changes in the economy, such as flexible land use policies and disaster-resistant infrastructure.

16.3.11. **A Focus On Health and Well-Being:**

- The quality of life for people is improved when health and well-being are given priority in urban planning. This includes taking into account factors like air quality, noise reduction, and access to healthcare.
- **Example:** *Copenhagen*'s emphasis on walking and bicycling not only lowers air pollution and noise from traffic, but it also encourages physical exercise, which improves the general health and wellbeing of its citizens.

16.3.12. **Data Analytics and Smart Technologies**:

- Monitoring and controlling urban systems with smart technology and data analytics increases productivity and raises the standard of services offered to citizens.
- **Example:** *Barcelona*'s smart city projects employ sensors and data analytics to control every aspect of city operations, from garbage collection to street lighting, making sure that services are effective and sensitive to the requirements of the populace.

In summary, for cities to be livable, inclusive, and resilient, human-centric design is crucial to urban development. Cities may improve the quality of life for their citizens by emphasizing the needs and well-being of its citizens, incorporating natural areas, encouraging mixed-use developments, guaranteeing accessibility, and utilizing smart technologies. Examples from cities such as Singapore, New York, Porto Alegre, Curitiba, and Copenhagen show how human-centric design concepts may be used to create dynamic and sustainable urban settings.

# Chapter 17: Collaborating for Success

## 17.1. Public-Private Partnerships

Public-Private Partnerships (PPPs) are cooperative agreements between governmental bodies and businesses in the private sector with the goal of funding, planning, carrying out, and managing services and projects that were previously supplied by the public sector. PPPs are crucial for utilizing the resources and strengths of both sectors to develop effective, creative, and sustainable urban solutions in the context of smart cities. Here is a detailed explanation of the function of PPPs in the development of smart cities, as provided by an IT and urban planning specialist, along with instances of successful partnerships:

17.1.1. **Development and Maintenance of Infrastructure**

17.1.1.1. **Transportation Systems:**

- **Example:** Private businesses handled maintenance and renovations as part of the London Underground's public-private partnership for infrastructure modernization, which resulted in notable gains in service quality and efficiency. Large-scale project delivery was made possible by businesses like Bechtel, which provided funding and experience that the public sector might not have been able to provide on its own.

17.1.1.2. **Smart Grid Technology:**

- **Example:** Xcel Energy and the local government in Boulder, Colorado, collaborated on the Smart Grid City initiative. The goal of this project was to build a fully integrated smart grid that would enable real-time management and monitoring of the distribution of electricity, hence increasing efficiency and reliability.

17.1.2. **Innovative Technology and Smart Resolutions:**

17.1.2.1. **Smart Lighting:**

- **Example:** To install smart LED street lighting, Los Angeles teamed together with Philips. This PPP used smart technology to modify lights based on real-time data, improving public safety and urban management, and it also produced significant energy savings and lower maintenance costs.

17.1.2.2. **Waste Management:**

- **Example:** Urbiotica, a private enterprise, collaborated in the development of Barcelona's smart waste management system. Utilizing sensors, the system minimizes operational expenses and environmental effect by optimizing collection routes and tracking garbage levels in real-time.

### 17.1.3. Transportation and Urban Mobility:

#### 17.1.3.1. Autonomous Vehicles:

- **Example:** Uber and the City of Pittsburgh collaborated to test and implement autonomous vehicles. Modern technology was able to be included into the city's transportation system because to this partnership, which also produced insightful data on the future of urban mobility.

#### 17.1.3.2. Public Transportation:

- **Example:** To create an integrated ticketing system, Stockholm's public transportation authority collaborated with the private company SL. This system makes it easier for people to use buses, trains, and ferries by using smart cards and smartphone apps.

### 17.1.4. Urban Development Sustainability:

#### 17.1.4.1. Green Buildings:

- **Example:** One of the best PPPs centered on sustainable urban development is the Hudson Yards project in New York City. In order to establish a sustainable urban environment, Related Companies and Oxford Properties devised the idea, which combines public spaces, smart infrastructure, and green building technology.

#### 17.1.4.2. Renewable Energy:

- **Example:** To research and execute renewable energy solutions, Siemens and Mitsubishi are only two of the many commercial partners involved in Masdar City, an Abu Dhabi planned city project. The city wants to serve as a center for sustainability and clean technology, demonstrating how PPPs may promote extensive sustainable development.

### 17.1.5. Connectivity and Digital Infrastructure:

#### 17.1.5.1. Broadband Access:

- **Example:** To create a gigabit internet network throughout the entire city of Chattanooga, Tennessee, the Electric Power Board (EPB) collaborated with private companies. This project promoted economic growth and drew new companies to the region in addition to enhancing internet access.

#### 17.1.5.2. 5G Deployment:

- **Example:** To implement 5G infrastructure, the City of San Jose collaborated with telecom firms like Verizon and AT&T. Through this partnership, next-generation connectivity was quickly implemented, improving the city's digital infrastructure and opening up a variety of smart city applications.

### 17.1.6. **Social and Health Services:**

### 17.1.6.1. **Telemedicine:**

- **Example:** To increase underprivileged people' access to healthcare, the City of Atlanta partnered with Philips Healthcare to develop telemedicine services. The PPP improved the standard and accessibility of healthcare in the city by offering cutting-edge medical services and technologies.

### 17.1.6.2. **Social Housing:**

- **Example:** To implement the Public Housing Renewal Program in Melbourne, the state government collaborated with commercial developers. With improved living conditions and social service integration, the goal of this initiative is to replace outdated public housing with brand-new, mixed-income communities.

### 17.1.7. **Economic Development and Job Creation:**

### 17.1.7.1. **Innovation Hubs:**

- **Example:** consider Toronto's MaRS Discovery District, a public-private initiative that has grown to become one of the biggest urban innovation hubs in the world. In order to promote innovation and economic progress, it encourages cooperation between startups, large enterprises, and public sector institutions.

### 17.1.7.2. **Urban Regeneration:**

- **Example:** A PPP between the UK government and private developers drove the London Canary Wharf redevelopment. With the help of this project, a run-down neighborhood was turned into a bustling business center that increased employment and the local economy by thousands.

In summary, partnerships between the public and private sectors are essential to the creation of smart cities. Public-Private partnerships (PPPs) have the ability to produce projects that improve urban infrastructure, enhance public services, and promote sustainable development by combining the resources, knowledge, and innovation of the private sector with the regulatory support and public interest emphasis of the government. A wide range of cities, including London's Canary Wharf, Los Angeles,

Barcelona, Pittsburgh, New York, Abu Dhabi, Chattanooga, Atlanta, Melbourne, Toronto, and London, demonstrate the substantial and varied effects of PPPs in developing intelligent, resilient, and livable urban places.

## 17.2. The Role of Communities and Citizens

Communities and their residents play a critical role in the success of smart cities. Involving locals in the design, construction, and administration of urban areas guarantees that initiatives are tailored to their requirements and preferences, promoting a feeling of empowerment and ownership. This is a thorough explanation of how residents and communities may work together to make smart cities successful, complete with real-world examples:

17.2.1. **Participatory Urban Planning:**

17.2.1.1. **Engaging Citizens in Decision-Making**:
- Participatory urban planning helps guarantee that development represents the true needs and preferences of locals.
- **Example:** As an illustration, participatory budgeting in Porto Alegre, Brazil, lets the public choose how much of the local budget is spent. Improved public services and infrastructure in underprivileged regions are among the urban development projects that have resulted from this effort, which also focuses on community equity.

17.2.1.2. **Crowdsourcing Solutions and Ideas:**
- Creative solutions to urban problems can result from utilizing the community's combined intelligence.
- **Example:** The Better Reykjavik platform in Reykjavik, Iceland, enables locals to suggest, debate, and select ideas for improving the city. The city council then puts good ideas—like new playgrounds and public parks—into action.

17.2.2. **Smart Initiatives Driven by the Community:**

17.2.2.1. **Regional Energy Initiatives**:
- Local energy production and management can be managed by communities, fostering resilience and sustainability.
- **Example:** Using blockchain technology, the Brooklyn Microgrid initiative in New York City allows locals to produce, sell, and purchase renewable

energy. This program encourages community involvement, energy independence, and clean energy use.

17.2.2.2. **Urban Farming and Community Gardens**:

- Initiatives led by the community to cultivate urban areas produce green spaces, support sustainability, and improve food security.
- **Example:** The urban farming movement in Detroit has turned abandoned lots into fruitful gardens, bringing inhabitants fresh produce and fostering a sense of community. Initiatives such as the Michigan Urban Farming Initiative also provide job training and educational initiatives.

17.2.3. **Improving Public Areas:**

17.2.3.1. **Community-Based Design for Public Spaces:**

- Public places that involve residents in their design and upkeep are more likely to reflect their needs and preferences.
- **Example:** the elevated linear park known as The High Line in New York City was created by significant community involvement and collaboration. A non-profit group called Friends of the High Line collaborates with the city and the neighborhood to manage and maintain the area, making sure it is always a popular public amenity.

17.2.3.2. **Placemaking Projects:**

- In order to improve the quality and usability of public spaces, Placemaking involves the community in their creation and transformation.
- **Example:** the *"Renew Newcastle"* project in Melbourne, Australia, brought local entrepreneurs and artists together to breathe new life into underutilized and abandoned houses. This neighborhood-driven project increased local involvement and economic activity by transforming run-down areas into vibrant cultural and commercial districts.

17.2.4. **Digital Involvement and Technology:**

17.2.4.1. **Data Collection and Citizen Science:**

- Citizens can help with data gathering and analysis, which can yield insightful information for managing and developing urban areas.
- **Example:** The Smart Citizen Kit was created in Barcelona and enables locals to keep an eye on things like noise levels and air quality. Citizens'

data collection ensures that environmental and city planning strategies are based on local realities.

17.2.4.2. **Digital Resources for Public Participation**:

- Direct communication between residents and local government is made easier by digital tools, which also improve responsiveness and openness.
- **Example:** The "mVoting" app in Seoul, South Korea, enables users to take part in surveys and polls on a range of urban concerns. This digital platform encourages more civic engagement and gives citizens the ability to influence policy decisions.

17.2.5. **Developing Social Resilience:**

17.2.5.1. **Support Systems and Community Networks:**

- Robust community networks augment social resilience by furnishing assistance in times of need and cultivating a feeling of unity.
- **Example:** The Student Volunteer Army in Christchurch, New Zealand, organized hundreds of volunteers to help with relief work following the earthquake. This grassroots effort showed the value of group effort and camaraderie in times of adversity.

17.2.5.2. **Initiatives for Cooperative Safety and Security:**

- Involving the community in safety and security projects improves efficacy and builds confidence.
- **Example:** the "Neighbourhood Watch" initiative, which is implemented in many cities across the globe, invites locals to collaborate with local law enforcement to keep an eye out for and report suspicious activity. By reciprocal vigilance and cooperation, this relationship contributes to the creation of safer communities.

17.2.6. **Cultural and Educational Projects:**

17.2.6.1. **Programs for Community Education:**

- Community-based education programs encourage civic engagement and lifelong learning.
- **Example:** the "Green Bronx Machine" in New York City teaches urban farming and sustainability to local residents and students. This program promotes community pride and environmental care in addition to imparting useful skills.

17.2.6.2. **Events and Cultural Festivals:**

- Cultural events organized by the community promote social cohesiveness and honor local traditions.
- **Example:** the community-organized "*Notting Hill Carnival*" in London honours the culture and legacy of the Caribbean. It fosters unity and understanding across cultural divides by bringing locals and tourists together.

In summary, through active participation in urban planning, leading local projects, improving public spaces, utilizing technology for civic engagement, fostering social resilience, and supporting cultural and educational events, communities and individuals play a critical role in the success of smart cities. The ability of community and citizen participation to create dynamic, sustainable, and responsive urban landscapes is exemplified by cities such as Porto Alegre, Reykjavik, Brooklyn, Detroit, New York, Melbourne, Barcelona, Seoul, Christchurch, and London. By including locals in this way, smart city projects are certain to be both technologically cutting edge and firmly anchored in the needs and goals of the communities they are intended to serve.

## 17.3. Global Collaboration and Knowledge Sharing

International cooperation and information exchange are critical to the development of smart cities. Cities all over the world may learn from one another's experiences, steer clear of common errors, and quicken the adoption of creative solutions by exchanging ideas, technologies, and best practices. Here is a thorough explanation of the significance of international cooperation and knowledge exchange, accompanied by specific examples:

17.3.1. **Global Alliances and Networks**

17.3.1.1. **Smart Cities Council:**
- The Smart Cities Council is a community of professionals and practitioners focused on smart cities that offers a cooperative forum for information exchange, resource sharing, and tool sharing.
- **Example:** The Smart Cities Council organizes the Smart Cities Week conferences, where global city leaders exchange case studies and deliberate on approaches for the advancement of smart city development. Smart city efforts from cities like Singapore and Copenhagen have been highlighted, providing others with insightful information.

17.3.1.2. **Global Covenant of Mayors for Energy & Climate:**

- **C**ities and local governments in this group are dedicated to sustainability and climate action.
- **Example:** through this network, the city of Paris, led by Mayor Anne Hidalgo, works with other international cities to exchange best practices for lowering carbon emissions and boosting urban resilience. Their climate action strategies and green infrastructure experiences serve as a model for other cities.

### 17.3.2. **International Collaborations and Projects:**

#### 17.3.2.1. **European Union's Horizon 2020:**

- Horizon 2020 is an EU research and innovation program that provides funding for projects that tackle a range of societal issues, including the creation of smart cities.
- **Example:** The Horizon 2020-funded Triangulum project includes cities such as Manchester (UK), Eindhoven (Netherlands), and Stavanger (Norway). These cities share best practices and outcomes as they work together to integrate smart grids, renewable energy, and sustainable mobility solutions.

#### 17.3.2.2. **Asia-Pacific Economic Cooperation (APEC):**

- APEC encourages information exchange and economic collaboration among Pacific Rim nations.
- **Example:** to address innovations and difficulties related to smart cities, industry leaders, researchers, and city officials from member economies come together at the APEC Smart City Forum. The discussion of subjects like data governance, urban mobility, and IoT integration promotes knowledge sharing within the area.

### 17.3.3. **Platforms for Sharing Knowledge:**

#### 17.3.3.1. **City Protocol Society:**

- An international group called the City Protocol Society creates guidelines and standards for projects involving smart cities.
- **Example:** cities like Boston and Barcelona work together to create and apply standardized solutions to urban problems through the City Protocol Society. This partnership contributes to the interoperability and scalability of solutions for smart cities.

#### 17.3.3.2. **C40 Cities Climate Leadership Group:**

- Megacities around the world who are dedicated to combating climate change are part of the C40 Cities Climate
- **Example:** The C40 network encourages the exchange of knowledge on climate action, with major cities such as New York, Tokyo, and London discussing approaches to cutting greenhouse gas emissions, boosting urban resilience, and improving air quality.

### 17.3.4. Collaborative Research and Innovation Hubs:

#### 17.3.4.1. Urban Innovation Labs:

- These spaces offer cities, scholars, and businesses a cooperative environment to create and evaluate novel urban solutions.
- **Example:** as part of the Amsterdam Smart City effort, tech companies, startups, and city officials work together on an innovation center where ideas like digital mobility solutions and smart energy systems are developed. Experimentation and quick prototyping are encouraged by this open innovation strategy.

#### 17.3.4.2. International Urban Cooperation (IUC):

- The EU-funded IUC program encourages city-to-city collaboration on sustainable urban development.
- **Example:** the IUC program combines cities from various regions to collaborate on common urban problems. For example, Chicago, USA, and Hamburg, Germany work together on sustainable urban mobility initiatives, exchanging information and ideas to enhance public transportation networks.

### 17.3.5. International Frameworks and Standards:

#### 17.3.5.1. ISO 37120: Sustainable Cities and Communities:

- This standard facilitates benchmarking and knowledge exchange by offering a set of metrics for quality of life and city services.
- **Example:** ISO 37120 is used by cities like Toronto, Canada, and Dubai, United Arab Emirates, to compare their performance to international standards, find best practices, and gain knowledge from the experiences of other cities.

#### 17.3.5.2. United for Smart Sustainable Cities (U4SSC):

- A United Nations program that aims to advance sustainable urban development on a worldwide scale.

- **Example:** through U4SSC, smart city frameworks, regulations, and technologies are shared by cities such as Vienna and Singapore. The program offers a venue for expanding on ideas and sharing best practices.

### 17.3.6. Exchanges in Scholarship and Education:

### 17.3.6.1. International University Collaborations:

- Universities from all over the world work together on cooperative initiatives and knowledge sharing related to smart city research.
- **Example:** the MIT Senseable City Lab works on projects that investigate the effects of digital technology on cities across the world, such as Singapore and Copenhagen. Their research results are disseminated throughout the world and impact smart city projects.

### 17.3.6.2. Online Courses and MOOCs:

- Massive Open Online Courses, or MOOCs, offer easily accessible instruction on the technologies and concepts of smart cities.
- **Example:** organizations such as the University of Illinois provide MOOCs on smart city subjects like IoT, urban data analytics, and sustainable urban planning. Global knowledge exchange and capacity growth are made possible by these courses.

In summary, global cooperation and knowledge exchange are essential to smart city development. Cities can benefit from the collective learning and experiences of the global community by taking part in international networks, cross-border projects, knowledge-sharing platforms, collaborating research hubs, adopting global standards, and holding academic exchanges. Instances from programs such as C40 Cities, Horizon 2020, Smart Cities Council, and others show the real advantages of these kinds of partnerships in fostering creativity, sustainability, and adaptability in urban development.

# Chapter 18: Conclusion: The Path Forward



We have investigated many aspects of smart city development as an IT and Urban Planning Specialist, from the incorporation of new technology to the significance of community involvement and international cooperation. Below is a summary of the main findings:

### 18.1.1. **New Innovations and Technologies:**

- Smart cities use blockchain, IoT, AI, big data analytics, and other cutting-edge technology to enhance urban living. These technologies facilitate improved public services, effective resource management, and real-time monitoring.
- **Example:** Barcelona's smart lighting system, for instance, shows how IoT may improve public safety and energy economy by adjusting brightness based on real-time data.

### 18.1.2. **Building Adaptive and Resilient Cities:**

- Constructing systems and infrastructure in smart cities that are resilient to a range of shocks, including natural catastrophes, climate change, and changes in the socioeconomic landscape, is essential to their resilience. This include encouraging sustainable urban development, strengthening disaster response capacities, and incorporating green infrastructure.
- **Example:** Tokyo's adaptable land-use rules and disaster-resistant infrastructure serve as an example of how cities can be built to change with the times.

### 18.1.3. **Human-Centered Urban Development Design**:

- The goal of human-centric design is to prioritize the needs and well-being of inhabitants while designing livable, inclusive, and accessible urban environments. This includes green spaces, sustainable design, mixed-use developments, and community involvement.
- **Example:** To create a lively, walkable area, the Carlsberg Byen project in Copenhagen blends housing, offices, retail, and cultural venues.

### 18.1.4. **Public-Private Partnerships (PPPs):**

- PPPs are necessary to fund and carry out initiatives related to smart cities. Through the synergy of public and private sector resources and knowledge, cities may effectively create novel solutions and infrastructure.
- **Example:** Los Angeles and Philips' collaboration to install smart LED street lighting has significantly decreased energy consumption and maintenance expenses.

### 18.1.5. **The Function of Citizens and Communities**:

- Planning and managing smart cities with communities and citizens involved guarantees that development meets their requirements and preferences. Residents gain a sense of empowerment and ownership as a result.
- **Example:** Reykjavik's Better Reykjavik platform enables residents to suggest and vote on municipal enhancements, resulting in neighborhood-driven urban development initiatives.

### 18.1.6. **International Cooperation and Information Exchange**:

- Cities may learn from one other's experiences, exchange best practices, and quicken the adoption of effective smart city solutions through international collaboration and knowledge sharing. Platforms for knowledge sharing, international networks, and cross-border initiatives are essential to this process.
- **Example:** megacities like London, Tokyo, and New York exchange methods for cutting greenhouse gas emissions as part of the C40 Cities Climate Leadership Group, which promotes knowledge sharing on climate action among these cities.

### 18.1.7. **Digital and Technical Infrastructure**:

- Smart cities are built on a foundation of strong digital infrastructure, which includes smart grids, 5G networks, and high-speed internet. The implementation of numerous intelligent services and apps is made possible by these technologies.
- **Example:** Chattanooga's PPP-developed citywide gigabit broadband network has improved internet access and aided in local economic growth.

### 18.1.8. **Sustainable Urban Transportation**:

- Reducing traffic congestion, pollution, and improving urban mobility require smart mobility solutions including integrated public transportation networks, electric cars, and bike-sharing programs.

- **Example:** Amsterdam's robust bike-sharing scheme and cycling infrastructure encourage healthier lives by lowering dependency on automobiles.

18.1.9. **Well-Being and Health:**
- When it comes to air quality, noise reduction, access to healthcare, and encouraging physical exercise, urban design prioritizes health and well-being. Residents' quality of life is improved by this.
- **Example:** Copenhagen's emphasis on walking and bicycling encourages physical exercise, lowers air pollution, and enhances public health overall.

18.1.10. **Social and Cultural Infrastructure:**
- The development and well-being of locals are supported by the integration of cultural and social infrastructure, such as community centers, schools, and medical facilities. Furthermore, artistic endeavors and cultural events promote a feeling of identity and community.
- **Example:** Melbourne's "Renew Newcastle" project has transformed deserted neighborhoods into vibrant cultural hotspots by reviving unused homes through community-led initiatives.

In summary, the future of smart cities lies on a comprehensive strategy that incorporates cutting-edge technologies, cultivates public-private partnerships, involves local communities, and encourages international cooperation. Cities may develop livable, inclusive, and adaptable urban settings that improve the quality of life for all citizens by placing a high priority on human-centric design, sustainability, resilience, and innovation. Effective instances from cities such as Barcelona, Tokyo, Copenhagen, Los Angeles, Reykjavik, and Melbourne demonstrate the possibilities and advantages of these approaches, providing important insights for the global advancement of smart city development.

## 18.2. Vision for the Future of Urban Living

In addition to being smart, sustainable, inclusive, robust, and able to adjust to the always shifting requirements of their citizens, smart cities are also anticipated to be resilient. I'm an IT and urban planning specialist, and I have the following comprehensive vision for urban living in the future, supported by examples:

18.2.1. **Sustainability and Care of the Environment:**

- In order to reduce their environmental impact, future cities will place a high priority on sustainability through the integration of green technologies, renewable energy sources, and circular economy concepts.
- **Example:** Masdar City in Abu Dhabi Masdar is a zero-carbon metropolis that combines wind, solar, and ecological building materials. Its all-inclusive waste management system sets the standard for sustainable urban development by placing a strong emphasis on recycling and composting.

### 18.2.2. Adaptive and Resilient Infrastructure:

- With infrastructure built to resist and adapt to natural catastrophes, climate change, and other disturbances, urban resilience will be a pillar.
- **Example:** Tokyo, Japan serves as an illustration of how a city may be ready for a natural disaster with its earthquake-resistant structures and cutting-edge early warning systems. Adaptive urban planning is best demonstrated by the city's vast flood control infrastructure, which includes the enormous subterranean floodwater diversion system.

### 18.2.3. Living and Human-Centered Environments:

- Cities will concentrate on developing livable, human-centered spaces that put citizens' enjoyment and well-being first. This entails creating public areas that promote participation with culture, physical exercise, and social contact.
- **Example:** consider Barcelona, Spain, where the "superblocks" project reclaims streets from automobiles to make them pedestrian-friendly areas that improve community spaces and lower pollution. This project serves as an example of how urban design may raise living standards.

### 18.2.4. Equitable and Inclusive Development:

- All urban dwellers, regardless of socioeconomic background, will have access to cheap housing, employment opportunities, and basic services in the future.
- **Example:** Vienna, Austria Vienna, renowned for its social housing concept, offers citizens decent, reasonably priced housing while maintaining social justice. The city is a worldwide leader in equitable urban development thanks to its inclusive policies and well-kept public housing complexes.

### 18.2.5. Intelligent and Networked Technology:

- Smart cities will streamline urban operations, improve public services, and increase overall efficiency by utilizing cutting edge technology like IoT, AI, and big data analytics.
- **Example:** Singapore, for instance Singapore uses a broad range of smart technologies as part of its Smart Nation plan, such as digital services that facilitate citizen-government interactions, intelligent traffic management systems, and a vast sensor network for real-time environmental condition monitoring.

### 18.2.6. **Integrated Urban Transportation**:

- Future cities will have smooth, multimodal transportation networks that give priority to environmentally friendly forms of transportation like walking, bicycling, and public transportation.
- **Example:** Copenhagen, Denmark Copenhagen is among the bike-friendliest cities in the world because to its vast bike network and cycling-friendly laws. Additionally, the city incorporates bicycle infrastructure into public transportation, making sustainable mobility practical and approachable.

### 18.2.7. **Well-being and Health Concentrated Design**:

- Public health and well-being will be prioritized in urban development, guaranteeing accessibility to green spaces.
- **Example:** The High Line in New York City, USA, is an elevated linear park that was constructed on top of a former railroad track. It offers a distinctive green area that encourages social contact, strolling, and recreation. The inhabitants' quality of life is improved by this creative reuse of urban infrastructure.

### 18.2.8. **Involvement and Engagement with the Community**:

- Urban planning and governance will be centered on active public interaction to make sure that development reflects the needs and ambitions of the community.
- **Example:** Reykjavik, Iceland, as an example. By enabling citizens to suggest and decide on municipal policies and projects, the Better Reykjavik platform promotes teamwork in urban governance. This participatory strategy guarantees that the planning and development of cities is directly influenced by the residents.

### 18.2.9. **Economic Vitality and Innovation Centers:**

- By assisting startups, varied industries, and innovation centers, cities will promote economic vitality and open doors for job creation and economic growth.
- **Example:** Silicon Valley, USA, as an example Silicon Valley, a global hub for innovation and technology, is a prime example of how towns can stimulate economic growth by supporting a thriving ecosystem of tech companies, research institutes, and startups. This concept draws talent from all over the world and promotes entrepreneurship.

18.2.10. **Digital Access and Inclusion:**
- For equal involvement in the digital economy and society, it will be essential to guarantee that every resident has access to digital technologies and the internet.
- **Example:** Chattanooga, TN Known as "Gig City," Chattanooga reduces the digital divide and promotes economic growth by offering all citizens access to cheap gigabit internet. The significance of digital inclusiveness is demonstrated by the city's investment in broadband infrastructure.

18.2.11. **Vibrancy in Culture and Society:**
- Future cities will use the arts, festivals, and inclusive public spaces that represent the distinct personality of the community to celebrate cultural variety and promote social vibrancy.
- **Example:** Melbourne, Australia, as an example A strong sense of community and cultural identity are fostered by the city's thriving cultural scene, which is bolstered by a number of festivals, public art projects, and community events. Melbourne's approach to cultural planning fosters social cohesiveness and enriches urban life.

In summary, urban communities of the future will be intelligent, inclusive, human-centered, resilient, and sustainable. Future cities may build environments that improve everyone's quality of life by integrating cutting-edge technologies, putting sustainability and resilience first, involving communities, and promoting economic vibrancy. The various and creative approaches to creating the cities of the future are exemplified by examples from places like Silicon Valley, Chattanooga, Melbourne, Masdar, Tokyo, Barcelona, Vienna, Singapore, Copenhagen, New York, Reykjavik, and Silicon Valley. This all-encompassing perspective guarantees that urban development is in line with people's changing needs and goals, resulting in lively, livable, and prosperous urban environments for coming generations.

## 18.3. A Call to Action for Stakeholders

Urban living in the future depends on the active engagement and cooperation of all parties involved, including communities, governments, businesses, and private citizens. Every stakeholder group is essential to advancing the transition of cities to ones that are inclusive, sustainable, and smarter. Here is a thorough call to action with examples for each group:

18.3.1. **Policymakers and Governments**:

18.3.1.1. **Clearly Define Your Goals and Policies:**

- For the development of smart cities, governments need to have a clear vision and strategic framework that includes laws that support inclusivity, resilience, and sustainability.
- **Example:** Singapore's government has set a complete vision for creating a *Smart Nation*, integrating technology into every element of urban life, from healthcare to transportation, and supporting this vision with well-defined legislation. One example is the Smart Nation Initiative in Singapore.

18.3.1.2. **Invest in Innovation and Infrastructure**:

- In order to facilitate smart city efforts, investments in both physical and digital infrastructures are essential. This covers smart grids, public transit, green infrastructure, and high-speed internet.
- **Example:** An illustration of smart city infrastructure is Barcelona, which has made significant investments in waste management, smart lighting, and Internet of Things infrastructure to establish itself as a pioneer in smart urban development.

18.3.1.3. **Develop Public-Private Collaborations:**

- To fully utilize the resources and experience of the private sector, governments ought to support and encourage public-private partnerships.
- **Example:** the city of Los Angeles and Philips collaborated to install smart street lighting, which significantly reduced energy use and enhanced public safety.

18.3.2. **Industry and the Private Sector**

18.3.2.1. **Create Innovative and Smart Solutions:**
- In order to solve urban difficulties, the private sector must lead innovation by creating cutting-edge technologies and solutions.
- **Example:** *Siemens* has created cutting-edge smart grid technologies that improve energy stability and efficiency in cities all over the world, promoting more sustainable urban settings.

18.3.2.2. **Collaborate with Public Sector:**
- To test and expand smart city initiatives, private businesses should aggressively pursue alliances with governments and other public organizations.
- **Example:** consider *IBM's Smarter Communities Challenge*, in which the company works with communities all over the globe to address urban problems pertaining to energy, public safety, and transportation by supplying knowledge and technology.

18.3.2.3. **Assure Inclusive and Ethical Procedures:**
- Companies need to follow moral guidelines, making sure that smart city technologies are accessible to all and safeguard private information.
- **Example:** consider *Microsoft's AI for Good Initiative*, which aims to create AI solutions that tackle societal issues, encourage moral AI practices, and guarantee that technology helps all facets of society.

18.3.3. **Academic and Research Institutions:**

18.3.3.1. **Conduct Research and Development:**
- When it comes to studying innovative technology, sustainable practices, and urban planning techniques, academic institutions are essential.
- **Example:** the *MIT Senseable City Lab* is a research center that works with cities all over the world to investigate how digital technologies affect urban life and provides creative answers and perspectives.

18.3.3.2. **Education and Training:**
- Colleges and universities should provide curricula and programs that give the upcoming generation of engineers, legislators, and urban planners the know-how to create smart cities.
- **Example:** The *University of Illinois' MOOC* on smart cities is one example. Accessible to a worldwide audience, this online course offers thorough

instruction on smart city concepts, technologies, and planning methodologies.

18.3.3.3. **Encourage Information Exchange:**

- The world should benefit from the information and best practices that are shared through academic conferences, publications, and networks.
- **Example:** the *IEEE Smart Cities Conferences* bring together policymakers, practitioners, and researchers to talk about the most recent developments and difficulties in the creation of smart cities.

18.3.4. **Society and Individuals:**

18.3.4.1. **Participate in Urban Planning**:

- To guarantee that urban development fulfills the needs and ambitions of the community, the community should actively engage in the planning and decision-making processes.
- **Example:** The *Better Reykjavik Platform* in Reykjavik enables locals to suggest and decide on city initiatives, guaranteeing that local demands are taken into account during the urban planning process.

18.3.4.2. **Adopt Sustainable Habits:**

- Locals can support sustainability initiatives by embracing eco-friendly habits like recycling, conserving electricity, and taking public transit.
- **Example:** consider *Copenhagen's Cycling Culture*, where people use bicycles as their main form of transportation, greatly lowering the city's carbon footprint and encouraging a healthier way of life.

18.3.4.3. **Encourage Change:**

- It is the responsibility of citizens to support laws and programs that advance inclusive, sustainable, and intelligent urban development.
- **Example:** *Grassroots Environmental Movements*, such as Greta Thunberg's Fridays for Future, are an example of how citizens may demand that their governments take more aggressive action against climate change.

18.3.5. **International Organizations and Non-Governmental Organizations (NGOs)**

18.3.5.1. **Encourage Community Initiatives:**

- Local projects that encourage resilience, sustainability, and community involvement can receive support from NGOs.

- **Example:** the *100 Resilient Cities Initiative* by The Rockefeller Foundation Through financing and knowledge, this program supports cities globally in developing their resilience to physical, social, and economic problems.

18.3.5.2. **Encourage International Cooperation**:
- International organizations ought to encourage cooperation and knowledge exchange between cities throughout the world.
- **Example:** *United for Smart Sustainable Cities (U4SSC)*, a program of the United Nations Through the provision of a forum for cities to exchange creative solutions and best practices, this program fosters international collaboration on the development of smart cities.

18.3.5.3. **Track and Assess Development**:
- NGOs and global organizations have the potential to track and assess the development of smart city projects, guaranteeing responsibility and ongoing development.
- **Example:** *World Bank's Global Indicators for Smart Cities*, for instance The World Bank creates benchmarks and indicators to evaluate the development of smart cities and offers data-driven policy recommendations.

In summary, all parties involved in urban living must work together to pave the way forward. While the private sector promotes innovation and moral behavior, governments are still need to provide leadership and make infrastructural investments. Communities must become involved and embrace sustainable practices, academic institutions must further research and teach the next generation, and non-governmental organizations (NGOs) should encourage and oversee development. Together, we can build inclusive, sustainable, and intelligent cities that improve everyone's quality of life. Collaborative efforts have the capacity to achieve this objective, as demonstrated by examples from Singapore, Barcelona, Los Angeles, MIT, Reykjavik, Copenhagen, and international projects like as the Rockefeller Foundation and U4SSC.

# Appendix 1: Frequently Asked Questions (FAQs)

## 19.1. FAQs about Smart Cities

The following is a list of Smart Cities' frequently asked questions (FAQs) and answers for easy of reference:

1.  **A Smart City: What Is It?**
    - **Answer:** *In order to effectively manage a city's resources and assets, a smart city combines Internet of Things (IoT) and information and communication technology (ICT). In order to monitor and manage traffic, energy, utilities, and other community services, data from people, devices, buildings, and other factors is processed and evaluated. For instance, Barcelona has installed energy-saving smart street lighting that modifies brightness in response to vehicle and pedestrian activity.*

2.  **What Are a Smart City's Primary Goals?**
    - **Answer:** *The main goals of a smart city are to boost urban services, encourage sustainability, stimulate economic growth, and improve the quality of life for its citizens. Smart Cities use technology to lower resource use, boost public safety, and increase citizen participation. For example, the Smart City program in Amsterdam aims to promote sustainable urban life by implementing green energy and smart traffic management technologies.*

3.  **In Smart Cities, Which Technologies Are Most Frequently Used?**
    - **Answer:** *A variety of technologies are used in smart cities, such as cloud computing, 5G networks, IoT sensors, Big Data analytics, artificial intelligence (AI), and Geographic Information Systems (GIS). Real-time data collecting and analysis for improved decision-making is made possible by these technologies. AI and IoT are used by Singapore's Smart Nation project to effectively manage traffic, urban planning, and healthcare services.*

4.  **How Is Transportation Enhanced by Smart Cities?**
    - **Answer:** *Smart cities enhance transportation through the use of smart traffic management systems, real-time updates for public transportation, and smart*

*parking options. These innovations facilitate improved traffic flow and congestion reduction. To cut down on emissions and travel time, Los Angeles, for instance, employs adaptive traffic control systems that modify signal timings in response to current traffic circumstances.*

### 5. In What Ways May Smart Cities Improve Public Safety?

- **Answer:** *Smart cities use predictive analytics, emergency response systems, smart street lighting, and security cameras to improve public safety. These tools support crime pattern analysis, swift event response, and public area monitoring. The Domain Awareness System in New York City combines information from sensors and video surveillance to give law enforcement situational awareness and alarms in real time.*

### 6. Which Projects Fall Under the Category of "Smart City"?

- **Answer:** *Some examples of Smart City initiatives are:*
    - ***Barcelona:*** *Water conservation, garbage management, and Smart street lighting.*
    - ***Singapore:*** *digital healthcare, smart homes, and driverless cars.*
    - ***London:*** *Smart traffic management and air quality monitoring.*
    - ***Dubai:*** *Blockchain-based commerce and Smart government services.*
    - ***New York City:*** *Smart Water management*
    - ***Amsterdam:*** *Smart Waste management*

### 7. In What Ways Do Smart Cities Encourage Sustainability?

- **Answer:** *Smart cities encourage eco-friendly mobility, waste reduction, the use of renewable energy sources, and the implementation of energy-efficient systems. San Francisco, for example, has smart trash cans that notify the city when they are full, streamlining collection routes and saving gasoline.*

### 8. What Difficulties Do Smart Cities Confront?

- **Answer:** *There are a number of obstacles to overcome, such as worries about data security and privacy, the high cost of implementation, the necessity for stakeholder participation and comprehensive urban planning, and technology compatibility. Robust cybersecurity protocols, long-term financing sources, and integrated planning strategies are needed to address these problems. For* *instance, the Sidewalk Labs project in Toronto had issues with data privacy and public pushback, underscoring the necessity of open and inclusive planning procedures.*

### 9. How Does Healthcare Get Better in Smart Cities?

- **Answer:** *Telemedicine, remote patient monitoring, health data analytics, and smart medical equipment all help to improve healthcare in smart cities. Better access to healthcare services, early disease detection, and individualized treatment strategies are made possible by these technologies. Smart healthcare solutions, for instance, enable prompt response to medical emergencies by enabling remote monitoring of elderly patients in Seoul, South Korea.*

### 10. What Part Do People in Smart Cities Play?

- **Answer:** *By actively contributing to community projects, offering input, and helping to develop smart technologies, citizens play a critical role. Their participation guarantees that the adopted solutions satisfy the requirements and preferences of the community as a whole. For instance, the "CityScore" program in Boston takes input from the general public to enhance municipal services and deal with neighbourhood problems.*

### 11. How Are Energy Resources Managed in Smart Cities?

- **Answer:** *In order to effectively manage energy resources, smart cities make use of smart grids, energy management systems, and renewable energy sources. These technologies make it possible to load balance, integrate solar and wind energy into the grid, and monitor energy consumption in real time. For example, Copenhagen wants to employ smart grids and renewable energy sources to become carbon neutral by 2025.*

### 12. How Do Smart Grids Help Smart Cities, And What Are They?

- **Answer:** *Smart grids are sophisticated electrical systems that effectively monitor and control the flow of electricity using digital technologies. They incorporate renewable energy sources, optimize energy distribution, and lessen power interruptions. For instance, the smart grid system in Chattanooga, Tennessee, has greatly decreased power outages and enhanced electrical problem response times.*

### 13. How Is Waste Management Addressed in Smart Cities?

- **Answer:** *IoT-enabled rubbish bins with sensors are used in smart cities to optimize collection routes and monitor fill levels. By predicting garbage generation trends, data analytics raises recycling rates and collection efficiency. RFID tags on trash cans are used by Seoul, South Korea, to better track and manage waste.*

### 14. What Role Does 5G Play in Smart Cities?

- **Answer:** *5G technology offers fast, low-latency connectivity that is necessary for Smart Cities' real-time communication and data transmission requirements. It facilitates the broad use of IoT devices and improves applications such as remote healthcare and driverless cars. For example, 5G aids autonomous car testing and allows real-time traffic control in smart cities like Shanghai.*

### 15. How Do Smart Cities Handle Problems Related to Water Management?

- **Answer:** *In order to effectively monitor water consumption, identify leaks, and manage water distribution, smart cities employ smart water meters, leak detection sensors, and data analytics. These innovations lessen water loss and help save water supplies. For instance, the Public Utilities Board in Singapore employs smart water sensors to identify leaks and improve water distribution management.*

### 16. Can Catastrophe Management Be Aided by Smart Cities?

- **Answer:** *Yes, early warning systems, real-time monitoring, and data analytics in smart cities improve catastrophe management. Drones, sensors, and communication networks are examples of technologies that offer vital information in an emergency, facilitating prompt resource allocation and evacuations. For instance, smart sensors in Japan provide citizens early notice of impending earthquakes so they can take preventative action.*

### 17. In What Ways Do Smart Cities Support Economic Expansion?

- **Answer:** *To entice businesses and investments, smart cities provide cutting-edge infrastructure, effective public services, and superior quality of life. Technology-driven advancements in waste management, energy, and transportation lower* *operating costs and promote an atmosphere that is favorable to business activity. As an example, the Smart Dubai program has increased corporate productivity and drawn a large number of IT and startup companies to the city.*

### 18. How Do Smart Buildings Fit into Smart Cities, And What Are They?

- **Answer:** *In order to maximize energy use, strengthen security, and increase tenant comfort, smart buildings employ automation, data analytics, and Internet of Things technology. They are essential to smart cities because they promote sustainability and energy efficiency. One of the smartest buildings in the world, The Edge in Amsterdam, for instance, uses Internet of Things (IoT) to monitor and manage heating, lighting, and workplace utilization.*

### 19. How Are Data Security and Privacy Protected in Smart Cities?

- **Answer:** *The implementation of strong cybersecurity measures, such as encryption, safe data storage, and access limits, is what smart cities do. To protect citizens' data, they also set up data governance systems and abide by laws like GDPR. For instance, the city of Barcelona has strict data protection laws in place and encrypts its smart city data.*

### 20. How Can Education Be Enhanced by Smart Cities?

- **Answer:** *Smart cities enhance education through data-driven insights into student performance, e-learning platforms, and smart classrooms. Better resource allocation and individualized learning are made possible by these technologies. For example, the Department of Education in New York City tracks student progress and customizes educational programs to meet individual needs using data analytics.*

## Table of Figures



## Bibliography


1. *"Smart Cities: Big Data, Civic Hackers, and the Quest for a New Utopia"; Anthony M. Townsend; W. W. Norton & Company (2013); ISBN: 978-0393082876*

2. *"The Smart Enough City: Putting Technology in Its Place to Reclaim Our Urban Future"; Ben Green; The MIT Press (2019); ISBN: 978-0262039673*

3. *"Smart Cities: A Spatialised Intelligence"; Antoine Picon; John Wiley & Sons (2015); ISBN: 978-1119075592*

4. *Mukosha Patrick; "Careers in Information Technology: Machine Learning Engineer"; (November 2023), GoodMan Series; ISBN: 9798224391813.*

5. *Mukosha Patrick; "Careers in Information Technology: Cybersecurity Analyst"; (October 2023), GoodMan Series; ISBN: 9798223274834*

6. *"Smart Cities: Cities of the Future"; Aniruddha Paul; Springer (2018); ISBN: 978-9811058427*

7. *"Smart Cities: The Future of Urban Infrastructure"; Vinod Kumar; Elsevier (2019); ISBN: 978-0128161692*

8. *"Against the Smart City"; Adam Greenfield; Verso Books (2013); ISBN: 978-1784780432*

9. *"Building Smart Cities: Analytics, ICT, and Design Thinking"; Carol L. Stimmel; CRC Press (2015); ISBN: 978-1482218298*

10. *"Designing Smart Cities: Rethinking the Urban Age"; Alessandro Aurigi and Nancy Odendaal; Routledge (2017); ISBN: 978-1138237373*

11. *"Smart Cities for Dummies"; David Batty, Peter Weill, and Stephanie L. Woerner; For Dummies (2020); ISBN: 978-1119545859*

www.ingramcontent.com/pod-product-compliance
Lightning Source LLC
Chambersburg PA
CBHW081142130726
47996CB00009B/2955